Tending God's Flock

Pointers for Pastors

David A. Boroughs

Preface

My writing of this book is an attempt to pass on what I
have learned during the thirty-seven years I have spent in
pastoral ministry. It is my heart's desire to be of help to
anyone who is called of God to be a shepherd to our Lord's
flock in a local congregation of believers. It is my hope
that perhaps some who read this book will find for
themselves a few precious nuggets that will enrich their
lives of ministry with the people of God. I also believe that
many of the challenges faced by pastors today are different
and perhaps more difficult than at any time before, as our
culture has moved progressively farther away from the
traditional norms and values of the past which were
influenced by a Christian perspective on reality.

This is not a researched or scholarly manual for ministers,
nor is it intended to be exhaustive in scope with regard to
the various facets of the work of a pastor. Rather, my aim
is to share what I hope is practical, helpful advice in a
conversational manner that is not laborious to read. The
suggestions and assertions contained in this book are my
own—someone else might advocate quite different
approaches to many of the issues and situations addressed
in this book. All I can say is that the advice given here
stems from what has worked for me, and the warnings
come from either things I did or have seen others do, that
proved to be ineffective, or detrimental.

This book grows out of my desire to be a link in the
learning chain for others in pastoral ministry. I have been
given much and greatly shaped by many Godly professors,
pastors, and other mentors, role models and saints from

whose experience and wisdom I have benefitted immeasurably. Now that many of those who were so precious and influential upon me during my earlier years have finished their race and are among the "great cloud of witnesses" (Heb. 12:1-2), I feel the responsibility to pass on to others anything I can that might lighten the load and be of value to those who shepherd the flock of God.

Sincerely,

David A. Boroughs

Table of Contents

Chapter 1

First Things First: Make Sure of Your Calling

We start with God's call because His divine plan for us is the fountainhead from which everything flows in our Christian lives. In all things His role is to initiate, and our role is to respond. The key to fulfillment and blessing as believers is that we hear and respond to God's continually upward call in Christ Jesus (Phil. 3:13-14). Since His call is foundational to who we are as believers and as God's servants, let's carefully consider the nature of God's call in the Christian's life.

All Believers are Called

I remember thinking as a boy that there were certain people who were "called," mostly pastors, evangelists, and maybe missionaries. I also remember hearing, usually at an ordination service, that "God's call to the ministry is the *greatest calling* one can have." While the particular men (almost all of them pastors) who made such statements were indeed Godly and sincere, I must say that I now believe those ideas to be only partially true. On the one hand, pastors, evangelists, and missionaries certainly should be called by God to their work, but *every believer* is also called. God calls all of us, when we hear the Gospel, to come to Jesus Christ, be saved from our sins, and surrender our lives to become His followers. He has a special plan for *each* of us. It is also true that there is no greater privilege than to be entrusted with the eternal Gospel which is "the power of God unto salvation to everyone that believeth" (Rom. 1:16). Certainly there are some whom

God intends to become pastors, evangelists, and missionaries, and that is great—for them.   However, all believers are entrusted with stewardship of the Gospel, and there are innumerable ways to bear witness to the saving grace of our Lord. As far as I am concerned, *whatever avenue of service God is calling you to* is the greatest calling you can have. If God is calling you to be a follower and witness for Jesus in the guise of a plumber, or a schoolteacher, or whatever, that's the *greatest calling*—for you!   The important thing is to discern what God has planned for you and to live it out.

I remember learning in the first grade, "No two snowflakes are just alike." Well, no two people are just alike, either. Each one is special and precious—made up of a unique combination of qualities ranging from hereditary and environmental factors, to personality, to natural talents, interests, and abilities.   Moreover, Christians are also endued with something more—*spiritual gifts*—imparted by the Holy Spirit who indwells every believer to equip us for service and witness. Nobody can be *you* like you can! Becoming the best version of that person God has created and redeemed *you* to be is God's greatest calling and should be your life's quest. Anything else means you're aiming too low!

The Experience of God's Call

The Bible gives us many examples of God's call as experienced by various people. For example, with Abraham (Gen. 12-24), known as "the father of the faithful," it is highly instructive that in the seven recorded encounters which Abraham experienced with God, there is a definite progression of His call on Abraham's life as God continually enlarges His original promises to Abraham as He beckons to him to step out a little farther and trust just a little more each time God appears to Him. While Abraham doesn't always do everything right—he fails some of the "daily quizzes" in the classroom of faith—he passes the "big test" (Gen. 22), demonstrating the preeminence of the Lord in his life up on Mount Moriah. The story of Abraham affirms not only the graciousness of God's call but also the continual, progressive, dynamic nature of His call in the believer's life. It's not a one-time thing. His call is a continual beckoning to us to let go of our "props" and to proceed a little further day by day along the pathway of a deepening faith relationship with Him in order that He may bless, develop, and use us more and more.

The call of Moses (Ex. 3-4), which includes the most glorious revelation of God's divine nature (YHWH, the One who is, was, and will be) in the Old Testament, serves to show us that, among other things, God's call is often experienced as one goes about his or her day-to-day routine of life and can happen even to one who is an outcast, rejected from society. God often intercepts us along the way, as later also happened with Saul on the Damascus road. Moses' encounter at the burning bush also illustrates how God often equips us beforehand with much of what we need to carry out his will, as shown in His question, "What is that in thine hand?" to which Moses replied, "A rod" (Ex. 4:2). It turns out that the shepherd's rod Moses already had was used in a mighty way numerous times in carrying out the task for which he was being called. This story also emphasizes that God's call to serve Him is lived out as we serve others, since Moses was to spend the remaining years of his life leading the children of Israel toward the land of Canaan.   Moreover, God's repeated promise of His presence, later demonstrated to all the people throughout the Exodus by the cloud and the pillar of fire serve to emphasize that God doesn't really call us just to work *for* Him but to be available for *Him to work through us*.

The call of Gideon (Judges 6:11-24) shows us that God does not see us as we see ourselves, illustrated by the fact that the angel of the Lord addresses Gideon as a "mighty man of valor" even though at that moment Gideon is threshing his grain by the winepress for fear of the Midianites. The first instruction to Gideon is to destroy the altar of Baal and the Asherah belonging to his father, which shows that responding to God's call will involve total surrender as well as a break with other loyalties, which previously dominated our lives. The tremendous response from several neighboring tribes of Israel when Gideon "blew the trumpet" illustrates that often many people are waiting and yearning for someone whom God has chosen to step forward and lead them. Gideon's putting the fleece out also shows the wisdom in seeking confirmation from God concerning His call rather than rashly charging ahead.

The call of Samuel (I Sam. 3) indicates that children as well as adults can experience God's call. In addition, little Samuel mistook the voice of God for that of Eli, the most Godly man he knew. It is significant that Eli recognized that God was calling Samuel before Samuel knew what was happening. Often older, wiser, more mature believers recognize what God may be doing in our lives before we ourselves can see it. The same truth is shown in the call of Elisha to be Elijah's helper and successor (I Kings 19:19-21).

Isaiah's experience of God's call in the temple (Isaiah 6:1-8) shows how God can use our circumstances to make us receptive, as illustrated by the fact that this encounter took place "in the year that king Uzziah died" (verse 1). While it is possible that this detail simply is included to locate the time frame in which God's call came, it seems more likely to me that, since Uzziah had reigned for 52 years, Isaiah may have entered the temple seeking God during a time of national uncertainty and transition. It is a fact that we all go through times when we are more receptive to God's call than at other times. As a beloved seminary professor of mine (now with the Lord) once said, "Anything is potentially revelatory!" The six-winged seraphim gave Isaiah—and us—a vivid example of how we should serve the Lord: with reverence (the wings covering their faces), humility (the wings covering their feet), and obedience (the wings with which they flew). Isaiah's "woe is me" (verse 5) in response to his glimpse of the HOLY ONE and the subsequent cleansing of his lips with a burning coal from the altar—the place of sacrifice—portray the graciousness of God's call as we consider that none of us are worthy of His care and attention. The question "Whom shall I send, and who will go for us," along with Isaiah's response, "Here am I; send me" make it clear that God desires a complete and open-ended surrender of the rest of our lives, although we do not know what the future holds. His warning to Isaiah that the people to whom he is being sent will largely ignore his message teaches us that true success in serving God is not gauged by the response of those to whom we are sent but by the faithfulness with which we serve—an important truth for us to keep in mind.

God's words to Jeremiah (Jer. 1:4-10) emphasize the sovereignty of the One who calls us, as the prophet is told that God's plan for him was in motion long before he was born. The call which we experience in our lives is the outworking of an eternal plan in which we are graciously included. His presence is the source of everything we need to carry out the task to which we are called, and we operate in the authority of the Transcendent One we are privileged to represent.

In the New Testament, the various accounts of Jesus' calling His disciples illustrate many of the same truths about God's call. His oft repeated words *"Follow me"* (cf. Mk. 2:14, et al.) show that His call is a continual, dynamic, relational, and transforming reality in the lives of those who join Him. His promise, "I will make you to become fishers of men" (Mk. 1:17 and parallels) shows the transforming nature of His call. The response of Simon and Andrew (Mk.1:18) and James and John (Mk. 1:20), along with Luke's statement that after the miraculous draught of fish that "they forsook all, and followed Him" (Lk. 5:10) give us a picture of the immediate and full surrender which His call requires. As the Synoptic Gospels unfold, the subtheme of the spiritual dullness of the disciples (shown in their slowness to grasp the meaning of Jesus' messiahship, the nature of greatness, their sleeping during the transfiguration, etc.) serves to demonstrate that He calls us not because of our ability but despite our inability. He patiently leads us along the path of discipleship, little by little transforming us—as we often respond in "fits and starts"—into miniature replicas of Himself called Christians.

In Acts 13:1-3 we have the account of the Holy Spirit moving upon the church to send Barnabas and Saul on the first concerted missionary journey. This Scripture emphasizes that the Holy Spirit made it clear to the whole gathering what He was calling Barnabas and Saul to do. This account demonstrates the importance of congregational confirmation of what we believe He is calling us to do, as we see the church's affirmation of God's call upon these men by their fasting, praying, laying hands on them, and then sending them forth.

So, from all these examples—and there are many others— we see that God's call can be experienced in the desert, in the temple, on a boat, while plowing a field, or threshing grain, or anywhere else, under any circumstance. God's call is tailored to fit each person and situation involved, and the ways it is experienced are as varied and unique as the individuals whom He calls. No matter how His voice is heard, the call of God is always gracious, life-changing, and full of blessing, though often requiring great sacrifice.

The Discernment of God's Call

In the Biblical examples above, each person "heard God's voice" in some manner. Most of them, especially the Old Testament characters, seem to have heard Him directly. Jesus' disciples were called personally by Him. Well, what about now? What about us? Part of being God is the sovereignty to do *whatever* He chooses. He *can* speak directly if He so chooses, but He *practically always* uses an avenue which was unavailable to most people during Biblical times—He speaks through the Bible. If I am unwilling to search the Scriptures under the guidance of the indwelling Holy Spirit in order to hear God speak it is highly unlikely that He's going to appear to me in some dream or a brushfire on the side of a mountain! Moreover, relying on some "vision" makes the basis of one's faith highly subjective, which in turn makes its reliability highly suspect. When you face persecutions or other trials you'll want to be sure you're building your life on something more substantial than some "dream" you had one night after you went to an exotic restaurant! If you're truly serious about discerning what God's will is for your life, God will use the Bible to help you find out, if you're willing to expend the effort to search its pages. He will also use other believers along the way to help you see what He's equipped you to do. His will is not some deep, dark secret He's trying to hide from you—it's something He yearns for you to know. That's why He created you and sent His Son to redeem you in the first place!

Of the many places in Scripture which address the subject of God's will, perhaps the key passage is found in Romans 12:1-2. Here is my translation of these two verses:

> I urge you therefore, brothers, through the compassions of God to present your bodies as a living sacrifice, holy, well-pleasing to God, which is your logical service of worship; and do not be molding yourselves in accordance with this world; rather, be undergoing transformation by the renewal of the mind, so that you may be proving what is the good, well pleasing, and consummate will of God.

In its larger context, these verses form a "hinge" in Paul's Epistle to the Romans, linking the doctrinal section (chapters 1-11), which spells out the Gospel message of justification by grace through faith, with the more practical section (chapters 12-16), which gives concrete ways for believers to live in response to God's gift of salvation. A strong argument can be made that most of the contents of chapters 12-16 could be viewed as commentary on these two important verses, so for our purpose it will be helpful if we consider some principles from this chapter relative to knowing the will of God.

First, there is the principle of surrender. Verse 1 urges us "to present your bodies as a living sacrifice" to God. If we are not yielded to God in our daily lives, there is no way we can ever know His "consummate will" for us. Let's think of the will of God as being like a superhighway with numerous lanes. On this highway are many cars, each headed off on its own journey, which represents the "consummate will of God" for that particular vehicle. In order to have any hope of getting to the right destination, each car has to first get on the road, leaving everything else behind. Once on the road, then it will be time for each driver to identify the proper lane toward the "consummate will" for that car. Getting on the road to knowing the will of God means you must make finding and following His plan your life's quest. We're talking *total* commitment. As long as you or I have another agenda to cloud our thinking we will never be able to recognize God's perfect will when He offers it. In this vein, there are some things God expects every Christian to do to get "on the road" and in the general direction of God's will. God expects *all* Christians to be involved in a local church, where we can experience meaningful worship which edifies, directs, and centers our lives in God's Word, where we can build relationships with other believers as members of Christ's body, and where our spiritual gifts can be discovered, developed, and used to benefit His Kingdom. God expects *every* believer to live a life of prayer and fellowship with Him. After all, He created us in order to fellowship with us. We ruined His plan for us by our sin, so He gave His Son to provide a way for our sin to be forgiven in order that we might have fellowship with Him again. God expects *every* Christian to study the Bible—the written record of His dealings with the human race and the story of

His unchanging love for us despite our rebellion against Him. Buried in the pages of Scripture is the will of God for your life, and He's ready to help you dig it out! God expects *every* believer to be a good steward of the material and financial resources He has entrusted to us. Demonstrating our recognition of God's ownership of both ourselves and our possessions will help us as ministers of the Gospel avoid the trap of viewing our work as a career rather than a divine calling, resulting in our seeking a congregation based on the salary and prestige to be gained rather than relying on His provision as we are willing to sacrifice. God expects *every* follower of Jesus to bear witness to the love of God he or she has found in Christ. I've heard it said that in our Lord's army there are no non-commissioned officers—we've all been commissioned to "preach the gospel to every creature" (Mk. 16:15). Doing these things that God expects all of us to do puts you "on the road" toward finding God's special plan for your life, but this is just the beginning if you want to really find the arena of service—the right "lane"—which He has prepared especially for you.

Next follows the principle of sacrifice. Jesus presented Himself as a sacrifice for us by dying on the cross, taking all our sins upon Himself, paying the ultimate penalty for all our sins. In response to what He has done, we are to present ourselves as sacrifices—not by *dying* but by *living* in sacrificial obedience to God.
Knowing and doing the will of God always involves sacrifice. Remember, Jesus said, "If any man will

come after me, let him deny himself and take up his cross and follow me" (Mark 8:34). God's perfect will is not something we can dovetail into our own agendas or fit into our schedule. *Our* plans must be willingly given up in the quest to find and fit into *his* plan. Each of us will likely face opposition and persecution, perhaps even from well-meaning people who simply do not understand. The bottom line is that it will cost all of us up front to follow Jesus. It's like a financial investment. We are constantly faced with the difficulty of choosing between spending our lives on what we want now or investing them in obedience to God with the prospect of an eternal reward later. Yes, it will cost us to find and do God's will, but failing to do so will cost us infinitely more.

Next there is the principle of giftedness (see verses 3-8). When we yield ourselves to be a "living sacrifice" by renouncing the world's values and adopting God's values, making it our life-long quest to find and fit in with His special plan for us, we begin to tap into the resources with which God has endued us to serve Him. These resources may be divided into three basic types. First, every person has natural talents. These include such things as being able to sing, play a musical instrument, draw a picture—anything which naturally comes easily to you. In addition, each person has interests—natural bents toward which our energy just seems to flow. Usually our interests lie in the same direction as our talents. The third category is unique to Christians— spiritual gifts. These are supernatural abilities for advancing God's Kingdom imparted to us by the Holy Spirit who came to live within us when we received Christ as our Lord. The New Testament gives us several sample lists of spiritual gifts, none of which I consider comprehensive. It is no accident that one of these lists occurs immediately following the two verses printed above. The point is that God's perfect plan for your life will involve your natural talents, your interests, *and* your spiritual gifts. He wants to use everything you are and everything you have. As mentioned earlier, no two snowflakes are identical, and no two believers are outfitted with exactly the same resources. You are a unique and precious individual whom God has gifted in a special way for a special kind of service. He has designed for you to have a unique opportunity to serve Him and be wonderfully blessed in the process—you do not want to miss it!

Next, there is the principle of community. Paul describes believers as members of "one body" (verses 4-5). Just as members of our physical bodies are interdependent and cannot function properly except in concert with one another, we are members of Christ's body and can only function properly as we cooperate together. This principle is crucial when it comes to discovering God's perfect plan for our lives. Here's how it works: What is good for you is also good for the whole church. The will of God for you will ultimately benefit the body of Christ, and it will deepen your involvement in His church. Active participation in the *koinonia* or spiritual fellowship of a congregation provides both a needed soundboard as well as a vital source of inspiration and power for service.   It is a fact that service and witness *must always* flow out of worship and fellowship in the body. Service and witness *can never* stand alone. So, whenever you feel like God may be leading you into any activity or ministry it is important to ask, "How will this benefit the body of Christ as well as the congregation in which God has placed me, and how will it affect my church involvement?" If it is good for you, then you should be able to recognize how it will benefit the church and your participation as a member of Christ's body. Likewise, the rest of the congregation should be able to see these benefits as well.   God's call in a person's life has both a personal and a corporate dimension. That is, if God has placed you here to be a pastor or whatever, other members of His body will also recognize this (cf. Acts 13:1-3). If you are struggling about your place of service, I would urge you to ask the wisest, most Spirit-filled Christians you know what they think God has equipped you to do in His body. They can give you some objective feedback concerning your gifts and abilities as well as help you see areas in your life in which you need to grow. If you are the only one in your church who thinks a particular avenue is the will of God, you're probably mistaken. On the other hand, if the most mature, spiritual Christians you know confirm what you think you are being led by God to do, then you're probably safe to proceed.

Finally, there is the principle of opportunity. If it is the will of God, He will provide a way to do it. That doesn't mean that the opportunity will come knocking on your front door tomorrow morning wearing a placard, but it does mean that God will give you a chance at it. He probably won't make it *easy*, but He will make it possible (cf. Mark 9:23). If you are living a life of surrender, presenting yourself daily as "a living sacrifice," renouncing the world and seeking God with all your being; if you are serious about being in tune with your giftedness from God for a particular area of service; and if you are functioning harmoniously as an active, healthy member of Christ's body, then you can be sure He will present you with the right opportunity to serve Him. Remember, just having a *feeling* that some activity or ministry is God's will doesn't mean that it is God's will. Rather, God's will is always molded in the crucible of self-sacrifice, it's always Scriptural, and it always benefits the church and will be affirmed by them. He also can be counted upon to provide us an opportunity to do it. Only when we are yielded to God can we—like Philip (Acts 8:26-40)—be in a position to recognize the chariot of God's opportunity when it comes rumbling by.

The Necessity of God's Call

It is important for every believer to respond to God's call, not only to receive Jesus as Lord but to allow Him to guide us into whatever avenue of service He has planned. However, for those of us who commit ourselves to devote our lives to the ministry of the Gospel it is *crucial* that we be sure that He has called us to this great work. In every arena of Christian service, we are endeavoring to fulfill a task which is humanly impossible—which only He can do. If I am in a form of service to which God has not called me, then my abilities, interests, and most importantly, my spiritual gifts will likely not be well suited for the work at hand, which will result not only in my frustration but also in the frustration of the recipients of my ministry attempts. Consider the kind of workmanship which would result if a mechanic tried to work on your car with only carpentry tools! Would you really want him to adjust your carburetor with a hammer? Or fix your flat tire with a saw? As silly as it sounds, I believe that sometimes people enter the Gospel ministry with good intentions (the road to destruction is paved with these, so I've been told!), maybe because one of their forbears was a preacher, or because "Grandma said I oughta," or it sounded like it would a good career. The effects can be catastrophic, not only for such misguided individuals but also for the unfortunate congregations that get them. Didn't Jesus say something about the blind leading the blind and both falling into the ditch (Mt. 15:14; Lk. 6:39)? We live in a time when it appears that more churches are "in the ditch" than ever before, and I wonder how much of it is related to people being in the ministry whom God did not call to that work. Even worse—there's a whole world of people not being reached because so much of the church's energy is being spent dealing with internal problems, some of it having to do with the wrong kind of leadership.

Another reason it is imperative that those who have surrendered their lives to the Gospel ministry be called of God is that sometimes the going can be so difficult that *only those who are truly God-called* can stick with it. When Satan "zeros in" on you and people start opposing and slandering you, or power brokers in the church decide to run you off—when "every which way" you turn you run into obstacles, the fact that you look "preacherly" when you wear a three piece suit or even that you went to the best seminary is not going to keep you from quitting. Every pastor I have known has at some time or another had to "go through the fiery furnace" of persecution or opposition within the church or in the larger community. Over the years, I have known many who gave up the ministry altogether, and some even fell away from the church. My heart goes out to each one, because I have tasted some persecution as well as considerable opposition in several of the churches I have served. I can tell you in all sincerity that if God had not made it *crystal-clear* to me that He has called me to pastor a church I would never have continued in it this far. I struggled long and hard for over a year about God's call before I surrendered my life to enter the Gospel ministry. When I did, it was because I knew that it was the *only* way I could be right with God. Shepherding a flock is a lot harder now than it was when I first started out (of course I was a lot younger then, too, and knew more!), and the world in which we live no longer has the respect for the church and its leaders that it formerly seemed to have.

As times become more difficult, it becomes more critical that we are clear about what God is calling us to do.

The Blessedness of God's Call

It is important that this chapter conclude on a positive, even joyful, note! There is *nothing* like finding and doing what God has placed you here to do! It is a true *"eureka!"* moment when you finally get really settled in your heart that *this* (whatever it may be) is what God is calling you to do! It really is like finding a buried treasure, or a pearl of great price (Mt. 13:44-46)! I can tell you right now, in spite of the difficulties, which have been many, if I had known how much God was going to bless me in response to His call, I never would have struggled so much in surrendering to it. Only that which He calls us to can really fulfill us! I thank Him for all the wonderful people He has brought into my life over the years! For the precious wife he gave me to help me in so many ways! (He let me pastor for five years as a bachelor, so I would *really* appreciate her when she came along!) I'm thankful for the fine churches He has allowed me to lead and serve, for the many people I've seen come to the Lord, for the many believers who've grown in Him, for the opportunities I've had to learn from them and grow with them, as well as for the close relationships I've been blessed to have with so many over the years.   I didn't recognize His call and yield to it because I'm so good; it was because *He* is so good that He gave me the opportunity. He also knew just how to get me to do it! I wouldn't trade any of the places, people, or experiences with which I've been blessed for anything. And even the hard times, and difficulties faced have all turned out for the best in the course of time (Rom. 8:28).

The mistakes I've made have been many, but even those have resulted in lessons learned and a deepening walk with Him as I am reminded I cannot do this alone. Whatever He is calling you to do, when you know what it is, go for it! Leap right into His arms!

Chapter 2

Reflection and Afterglow: Your Walk with God

As the moon is designed to reflect the glory of the sun, illuminating the earth during the night, believers are intended to reflect the glory of God, illuminating this spiritually dark world. Like the moon, which continually goes through its 29 ½ day cycle from new moon to second quarter to full moon to last quarter to new moon again with the shadow of the earth blocking varying degrees of sunlight from reaching the moon, we go through "phases" in our spiritual lives in which the world comes between us and our Lord and casts its shadow over us so we can only receive and reflect varying degrees of His light. As is the case with the new moon, the world may almost totally block His glory from us from time to time, while at other times we may break free from the world's shadow for a season, as during the full moon. This analogy breaks down somewhat when we consider that the lunar phases are continuous and follow a regular and predictable plan, just as He has assigned a particular orbit or path for the moon and the earth to follow, with the sun remaining constant. He has a designed a path for us as well, but He allows us the freedom to make choices as to whether we follow that path. We decide day by day when, how, and to what degree we will allow the world to come between ourselves and our Lord. The moon automatically becomes full each month, but if we ever experience that "full" phase in our Christian lives it is because we have consciously and fully surrendered to Him and have willingly renounced the shadow or influence of this world during that time. While it is nice to think about how we ourselves can be blessed with the fullness of His glory shining upon us, the ultimate beneficiaries will be those around us whose darkness can be dispelled by His glory reflected from us. As with Abram (Gen. 12:2), God's desire is not only for us to be blessed but also to *be* a blessing to others! Therefore, it is vitally important for all believers, and especially those called to the work of "equipping the saints for the work of ministry" (Ephesians 4:11-12) to maintain a close walk with the Lord, so we can reflect His light upon others.

 Let's consider another picture. After Moses had dealt with the children of Israel's rebellion and idolatry with the golden calf in Exodus 32, he then unselfishly interceded on their behalf in chapter 33 and finally secured the Lord's promise that His presence would once again accompany Israel on their journeys. Then Moses pleaded, "I beseech thee, show me thy glory" (33:18). The Lord's response was to grant him a second 40 days up on the mount, a replacement set of stone tables containing the Decalogue, renewal of the covenant, followed by an experience of God's glory—as much as Moses could handle—being safely shielded in a crevice in the rock. Verse 29 tells us that when he descended from the mount, Moses had no idea that his face shone with the afterglow of what he had just experienced. What a picture of how the ministry should be! Unknowingly, Moses glowed with the radiance of God's majesty, the glory of His holiness, the light of His truth, along with the warmth of Moses' own satisfied soul. God ratified His covenant the first time (Ex. 24:9-11) by granting a theophanic revelation to Moses, the priests, and seventy elders—and the covenant was broken even before Moses got back down the mountain with the "hard copy" of the Ten Commandments. This time the renewed covenant is ratified by God's revelation *through Moses' face!* When the Israelites see Moses, they see the reflected glory of the One with whom they have to do! God uses this glow to confirm Moses as the leader of His congregation, and to authenticate for His people that the truth given through Moses comes from God Himself. Oh, that His congregations today might see His glory radiating from their leaders who have just come to them after meeting with Him "on the mountain!"

From what you've just read, I hope you can already see my point: your own personal walk with and experience of God is the most important ingredient in serving our Lord and in leading His people. This is *especially* true in pastoral ministry. When your congregation knows that whenever you step into the pulpit, or enter the homes of the bereaved or the hospital rooms of the sick you have just "descended from the mount" with the afterglow of His glory radiating from your presence, they, like the religious leaders who wanted to silence Peter and John (Acts 4:13) will take notice of you, that *you have been with Jesus!* Ministry is not so much about what we do for the Lord; rather, it's what the Lord does in us and through us. Therefore it is imperative that we take the time to devote ourselves to the Lord, and to pray and search His Word for our own personal inspiration and guidance in our day-to-day lives. We cannot lead anyone else down the path of discipleship farther than we ourselves have gone, and we cannot impart to anyone else what we ourselves do not have. The more He gains our full attention and surrender, the more He is able to not only "shine upon us" and fulfill us but also to bless others as He is reflected through us. And in the process, the more like Jesus we become.

As great as the demands can be on a pastor, it is imperative that we carve out space in our lives for prayer, study of the Scriptures for our own enrichment, and time to be alone with God. We who are entrusted with the care of our Lord's flock need to be sure our spiritual wells do not run dry. It is extremely easy to become so involved in church work, committee meetings, ministry to those with special needs, crisis situations which come up, funerals, as well as preparation for preaching and teaching that we neglect our own spiritual lives. One of the common struggles for pastors is that if we're not careful we find ourselves looking for sermon material every time we open the Bible instead of listening for God to speak to us concerning our own individual needs. It is a good practice for pastors to be continually making a personal study of some book of the Bible for our own enrichment and spiritual vitality. It may well be that months or even years later the Lord will burden your heart to preach a series of messages or lead in a study of that particular book of Scripture. When that has happened to me, it has carried with it the added advantage of my having had several months or even years for the message of that book to sink deeply into my heart and produce a real effect on me as it has taken root in my life. Then I've been able preach or teach with much greater effect from the overflow—and afterglow—of that which God has used to move and to shape me. There is also much for pastors to pray for—the lost, the wayward, the suffering, the sick, the bereaved, and so on. Therefore, it is easy to become so caught up in intercession that we can neglect our own need to just bask in His presence for its own sake. It is so important to find a way—whatever way fits you—to get alone with Him on a daily basis. That's how our batteries are recharged so we can glow brightly!

The Bible is replete with our Lord's promises of His continual presence with us through the indwelling Holy Spirit. Believers are called to a life we are unable to live and to a work we are unable to perform—but He is able! When we fully surrender ourselves to be available for Him to control us, He is able to live the Christian life in us and through us! This doesn't mean that we can be idle, or fall into some kind of "trance" as He somehow "takes over" while we "take our minds out of gear." To the contrary, He wants to take control of every part of us, including our energy, abilities, time, and other resources, so He can not only bless us, but also meet the needs of others through us and through our efforts. We become what Paul refers to as "co-laborers with God" (I Cor. 3:9). What a privilege to be involved in a partnership with the One who has no shortage of resources at His disposal. He didn't have to come here in the person of Jesus Christ and pay for our sins on the cross, but He chose to do that because He *loves us!* Talk about grace! He knows all about us, and He *still* wants us! And He wants everyone else, too! Just as God flagged Moses down with a common thorn-bush ablaze with His presence, though not destroyed by it, He wants to set us afire with His glory to attract others to turn aside from what they're doing to meet Him. It's a cooperative effort involving Him and us, with God being the larger of the two parties. Although it takes a total investment on our part, His part is much greater, since He came here in the person of Jesus Christ, was crucified for our sins and rose again, and has imparted His Holy Spirit to transform, lead, empower, and bless everything involved in this process. What a miraculous plan to be part of, and what a marvelous God we serve! Therefore, it is crucial that we stay close enough to His presence to be ignited with His glory, in order that others may see Him.

Chapter 3

Sharpening Your Axe: Preparation for the Task

"If the axe is dull and he does not sharpen its edge, then he must exert more strength" (Eccl. 10:10 NASB).

I have used an axe as well as a chainsaw many times during my life, not to mention an assortment of other cutting tools during the years when I was a carpenter. One of the secrets to the effective use of such tools is to make sure they are *sharp* before you start to work. Incidentally, I remember hearing it said that the only edged tool that becomes sharper with use is the tongue! But speaking of sharpening the tool before using it, I can remember thinking soon after surrendering my life to God's call to preach the Gospel that all I needed was "a church in one hand and a Bible in the other!" Having struggled for more than a year with His call in my life, now that I knew for sure what I was supposed to do I couldn't wait to get started! Thank God for His providential hand that arranged for so many things to fall into place, so I could get the preparation I really needed! At 28 years of age, I had been a carpenter for 12 years, working with my father and gaining skills and knowledge—besides building my own house—which have stood me in good stead ever since, both for doing handyman and mission projects and supporting my family during a few times we were between pastorates. I also found myself doing carpentry for a few years when Jennifer and I were church planters, part of that time with no ministry salary. I believe it is a good thing for any pastor to have some other marketable skill other than preaching— just in case. (I've often thought that it might be helpful if a seminary education could include some kind of introductory course along that line, maybe calling it "Tent-making 101!") After surrendering to His call, God did not immediately give me a church to pastor, but within six months I became the interim pastor of a church near where I lived. After another six months this same church called me to be their pastor.

During this time, God placed several people in my life that encouraged me to further my education in preparation for the ministry. At the time, I only had a high school diploma. Also, I was not yet married—without even a prospect! I loved to read and study, but at first I thought I really did not need much formal education. After all, I had been working every day since high school, and I could find out anything I needed to know on my own. I remember the Director of Missions in the association to which my new church belonged telling me that one of the best things a higher education would do was to help me "learn how to think." Of course, I considered myself to be pretty good at that already! I guess the problem with ignorance is that you really *don't know* what you don't know! It turned out that the six months God allowed me to serve as interim pastor before actually becoming pastor of my first congregation was a time of great realization on my part. It didn't take very long for me to realize that I needed not only to know more but also to know *how to go about* many more things than I had realized would be involved. Therefore, part of the agreement by which my first church called me as their pastor was that I would begin commuting back-and-forth to college as a ministerial student the next fall.

When I started as a college freshman at the ripe old age of 30, I only intended to try to go as far as earning a bachelor's degree—if I could just keep from flunking out! It turned out, however, that being a little older and having a strong work ethic along with a sense of mission gave me the focus that enabled me to do quite well. In fact, the Lord opened the doors for me to later earn seminary degrees at the master's and doctoral levels. These privileges have proved to be absolutely *priceless*, and not only my ability to serve Him has been expanded, but my very life itself has been enriched in so many ways by this time of preparation. Being in the learning environment of a university stimulated me in a myriad of ways I never could have imagined. Already being a pastor meant I had a "proving ground" for all the new things I was learning. (There *has to be* a special reward in heaven for first churches, especially mine!) Also, practically everything I was learning was immediately *relevant*. Well, maybe not quite—I think algebra mostly helped my prayer life! Still, for the reasons that follow, and more, I wouldn't trade one minute of the time I spent at any of the three fine institutions of higher learning I have been blessed to attend for *anything* in this world.

One of the most valuable benefits of a theological education is that you not only learn *about* theology, you learn *how to do* theology. When I began, I figured a theological education meant I would have "a box of answers" to all the questions I would be asked as a pastor. Then in a class one day during my first year, a saintly professor, now with the Lord, made this statement which has always remained with me: "A theological education is not nearly so much about getting all the right answers as it is about asking the right questions." Gradually, I came to see that I was not going to be given a theology; rather, I was going to have to, as it were, "work out my own salvation with fear and trembling" (Phil. 2:12). Rather than being handed the finished product, I was provided with a set of tools and given guidance in developing the skills with which to fashion my own. It took time, but more and more I came to realize that a *real* education, while it does include learning a great deal of information about many subjects, is not primarily about finding out all you'll need to know so you can then go out and apply it. Rather, a real education is about developing skills that will help equip you *for a lifetime of learning.* It is sad but true that there are some so called "seminaries" and "theological schools" which specialize in the indoctrination of students into a particular set of views, usually to fit into some kind of denominational mold. It is also worth saying that some of the professors from whom I really learned the most were the ones with whom I disagreed the most. They challenged me to not only be sure of *what* I believed, but also to consider *why.* The best schools, by far, are the ones that, as I was told early on, help you "learn how to think."

Another important benefit of a theological education is the opportunity you receive to have the privilege of studying under the tutelage of Godly professors and come under the influence of their knowledge, wisdom, and experience. Many of those from whom I learned so much became my mentors, role models, counselors, and close friends. Some of these professors had given prior years of their lives to serving the Master as pastors; some as missionaries in distant lands, while others spent most of their adult lives teaching in the classroom. As the years have gone by, I have in varying degrees kept up with several of these former professors of mine to whom I owe so much. If I ever amount to anything as His servant, it will in large part be due to the way He has used them in my life. The only way I can repay them is to try to pass along to others what I have been given. If I can be a link in someone else's chain of learning, then all that has been entrusted to me will not have been in vain. Now that so many of them have gone on and are part of that "innumerable multitude" around the Throne, I am continually inspired by my memory of their faithfulness to remain steadfast in serving my Lord, hoping to one day hear Him say to me, "Well done!"

A third immeasurable blessing to be derived from a theological education is from the relationships which you can develop with fellow students, who later will become your colleagues, confidants, and life-long friends in ministry. There is a special bond which develops among students who are making preparation side-by-side for their God-called life's work. My two best friends today were each fellow students with me at different periods during my years of school, and our friendships have grown to the point that our wives and children are also very close. We are family. There are also many others whom I still count among the most precious and influential people I have ever known, though we have gone our separate ways and may not have seen each other for years. Now that many years have passed since I first set foot on a university campus as a student, I can honestly say that one of the greatest blessings I received during my ten years of higher education was the friendships formed and memories made with fellow students. Several of these friends have been valuable sources of wisdom and advice as we have talked, struggled, and prayed together over situations which have arisen in one or the other of our ministry situations. Such supportive relationships are crucial if one hopes to survive long in the ministry.

In the long run, you can cut more wood in less time (and with more efficient use of your energy!) if you take time to sharpen your axe first. Preparing for the ministry by putting enough time, money, and sweat into getting a good theological education is an investment which is not only worthwhile, it is a necessity if one hopes to be used of God to the greatest possible advantage. Taking a shortcut will only make the journey more difficult and slower. If you don't sharpen the axe first, you must exert more strength. Remember, God's call to service is also a call to preparation. It's a worthwhile and necessary investment which will produce great dividends.

Chapter 4

They Only Have You:
Prioritizing and Protecting Your Family

Many are the demands upon a pastor's time and energy. A wise layman in a former pastorate once told me, "You only have so much energy, so you need to be sure to use it where it will do the most good." The fact is, in the ministry one does not always have the luxury of choosing where one's energy will be spent, since it is the very nature of ministry that needs and crises can arise as suddenly as storms on the Sea of Galilee. At practically every church gathering, the pastor will learn of some need, maybe a sickness or death within or connected to the congregation which may require some immediate response on the pastor's part. At deacon ministry meetings, which are usually monthly, and at church staff meetings, which may be weekly in multi-staff congregations, more needs will surface, not all of which necessarily require your personal attention, particularly if a deacon or other staff person is already responding. Nevertheless, it quickly becomes quite a lot to keep up with. Then when you factor in all the committee work, worship planning, and outreach coordinating, it is quite easy for the whole week to be filled to overflowing with church work, with your family making do with whatever may be left over. You cannot afford to let this happen! Your spouse and family will often be your only safe haven! They see and understand you as no one else does. Therefore, you must make the time to build strong relationships with your spouse and children. Above all, remember this: *They don't have a pastor!* They only have *you*, so you'd better make sure they get the best part, not the leftovers.

As I look back over the past thirty-seven years spent serving seven different established congregations plus planting one other church, I can truly say that many are the frustrations for a pastor. A drill sergeant gives an order, and the recruits are required to obey. However, as a pastor you are working primarily with a group of volunteers, and they always have the option of doing something else or staying home altogether. Many are the times when people in a congregation will seem excited about some new ministry or outreach project only to fail to support it with their time, energy, and resources when the actual work begins, especially if visible results are not immediately forthcoming. In addition, the Enemy, who seems to always work overtime, often arouses opposition either directly or behind the scenes in response to whatever you are trying to do. I guess every Nehemiah must contend with a Sanballat and a Tobiah (they really do seem to come in pairs!) who are bent on hindering us from carrying out the work to which we are called, so that "the strength of the bearers of burdens is decayed, and there is much rubbish; so that we are not able to build..." (Neh.4:10). In most kinds of work one is able to see and measure in some tangible way what has been accomplished when the day is done. However, in the ministry we are working to influence and change human lives with the Gospel of Christ in the power of the Holy Spirit; consequently, much of the fruit being produced is gradual and not easily measured. Remember Jesus' parables of the Kingdom (cf. Mt. 13)? Our work is a lot like farming—you do a great deal of planting, cultivating, watering, and waiting—often not noticing many visible results. All this involves tremendous investments of time, sweat, prayer, and mental and emotional stress as we give ourselves to this great task. The results come in God's time and in His way. Then again, some of the fruit we think we see being produced seems to suddenly die on the vine, or some of our "wheat" turns out to be "tares," as people we invest ourselves in for ministry or soul-winning, like Bunyan's "Pliable," are often easily led back down the wrong path once again. The pastor's heart must bear many burdens, a large portion of which are confidential and wouldn't be understood even if people knew. Keep in mind, being a shepherd is quite different from being one of the sheep. Again, your family is your safe haven. Not only do they see you and understand you as no one else does—they have a window into your life that no one else does, which enables them to see what a struggle it can be to shepherd a flock. Most of all, *they love you as no one else does!* Sooner or later, the day will surely come when you look out across the congregation during a time when the "fiery furnace" is seven times hotter than usual, and you'll realize that the only people you can *really count on* is your spouse and family. They'd better be getting the best you have to give.

It is also true that there are many challenges that a pastor must face even when things are going quite well in the church. There is always more that needs to be done, and part of being a shepherd is envisioning where "the green pastures" are and leading your flock in that direction. What this really means is that pastoral leadership is largely about being an agent of change, which always involves helping people to move out of their comfort zones. As mentioned earlier, your congregation—your work force—is made up of volunteers. You may really have a clear vision of where your congregation needs to be, as well as a workable strategy for how to get there, but unless they catch that vision and buy into the plan your flock may still be grazing on the same little familiar shady spot with dead grass this time next year. One of the most important things you can do is to enthusiastically, clearly and repeatedly communicate your vision to them—but what a challenge that is! Enthusiasm is contagious but costly—it takes a great deal of energy. But the fact is, if you're not sold on your vision no one else will be either. Again, to be clear requires you to maintain a finely tuned focus—which also takes a tremendous amount of energy as well as determination to keep from being turned aside in another direction. Moreover, repeatedly holding forth your vision carries with it the risk that both you and your vision will become boring, (it's an extension of yourself) unless you can continually find fresh ways to express what "the promised land" will be like. Another ingredient and challenge in helping your congregation catch your vision is that it works best if *they* help formulate the vision as well as the strategy. This means that whatever the actual plan ends up being it will have their fingerprints on it as well as yours, and it may be quite different (and probably not as bold) as what you would really like to do. Shepherding a flock means you have to find a way to balance between those sheep who are easily led and like to walk fast and those who are less motivated and want to move slowly or not at all. You have to keep your flock together, and you have to keep them moving forward, but usually at a slower pace than you would like. These are just a few of the many challenges you face. Here again, your spouse and your family is your sheltered harbor. They not only understand you and love you more than anyone else does, *they believe in you as no one else does!* This should become more and more true as the years go by and as more and more situations are faced together—but only if you invest yourself in building strong family relationships which grow through the years. Remember, your family is in the ministry with you, no way around it, and they deserve the very best you have to give.

It should also be clear by now that there are many sacrifices that a pastor *and family* must make in order to be effective in ministry over the long term. Jesus urged would-be disciples to "count the cost" and gave many warnings with regard to how worldly entanglements and divided loyalties can hinder us from following Him. His most pointed portrayal of the demands of discipleship included self-denial and cross bearing (Mk. 8:34-38). If this is true for rank and file followers of Jesus, it goes double for those whom He has called to shepherd His flock. Most who surrender to God's call to enter the ministry have at least some understanding that there will be certain things that must be renounced to fulfill this calling, but it usually turns out there are other unforeseen sacrifices which also must be made along the way.

Remember God's words in the Garden with regard to Adam being alone? "Not good!" (Gen. 2:18). I served as a pastor for close to 5 years before I was married. Maybe God waited so long to bring me a wife, so I would be sure to appreciate her after He brought her to me! I had so many more limitations in the ministry when I was single! Just as one small example, during my first or second year as a pastor I was wearing a new suit one Sunday, and as I greeted the departing members of the congregation it was pointed out to me that there was a tag hanging from one of my sleeves! Looking back, I'm sure there were other times my socks did not match. Actually, not too long ago I wore two black shoes from different pairs on a Sunday morning! Jennifer noticed when I got into the car with her to go home! A few members did in fact notice, but they said they assumed I must have hurt one of my feet and needed a more comfortable shoe on that (which?) foot! When I told the congregation Sunday night what I had done, everyone had a great laugh. Incidentally, this is a great place to repeat the words of a saintly preaching professor from my seminary days, "Your humanity is your best asset in the pulpit!" I guess I received a double portion! However, the wife God gave me has proven to be indispensible in countless wonderful ways in ministry, over and above helping me look presentable on Sundays. God has given her an incredible discernment with regard to people, which I can only attribute to the Holy Spirit at work in her life for my/our protection.   It's probably true that part of this is due to the fact that as a woman she's "wired" differently than I am as a man, but she has such an ability to "read" people that I have learned to always listen to her, particularly when she spots a potential "problem person" or one with a hidden agenda around whom I'll need to be careful. God has used her time and time again to keep me out of entanglements in problem situations of all kinds. She and my daughter have followed me from one church to another over and over.   We have never served a congregation that paid enough so that Jennifer did not have to work. Every time we've moved, she's had to find a new job—and start over again at the bottom, which she has cheerfully done. I would be lost without her! She and my daughter (now grown up and on her own) deserve the very best I have to give. I'm all they have, and they're all I have!

Chapter 5

When God Opens a Door: Finding a Fertile Field

I can remember as a young boy being told that when I met the right girl whom I was supposed to marry I would "just know!" While it was indeed true that years later after I met Jennifer I did "just know," I distinctly remember how *unhelpful* it was to me at the time to be told that. I wanted to find out *how* I would know—I guess I wanted some kind of checklist or at least a set of clues to look for! But no! All I was told was that I would "just know" –and she would, too! How similar are the dynamics involved in finding the right marriage partner with those involved in finding the right congregation to pastor. In both endeavors, there are no hard and fast rules—things often seem to "just happen!" However, there are a few things one can do which will greatly help along the way.

First, it is important to remember the priority of prayer. This cannot be overestimated, whether one is seeking God's choice of the right spouse or His choice of a congregation to serve. Just as the potential life partner is out there somewhere walking around on the earth at this very moment, so the congregation God would have you to shepherd is there, and *He knows all about it!* Therefore, it is imperative to stay in tune with God in your search. You may have in mind a particular "ideal church" that you envision serving; however, God knows what you both really need. That does not mean that nothing you envision is valid. Rather, your plans must remain tentative and your aim flexible. For one thing, just as there is no perfect pastor, there is no perfect congregation. The miraculous thing is that our Lord is able to take flawed people He has called and match them up with flawed congregations in a way that can bring mutual fruitfulness and fulfillment. For this to happen, the Holy Spirit must be allowed to lead, and the most critical component in this process is prayer. It also follows that the potential congregation looking for a pastor should also be given to prayer for His leadership. When we devote ourselves to prayer about a potential field of service, we open the door for the Holy Spirit to mold our thinking to fit His plan for us, enabling us to then recognize the right opportunity when it comes. When the union of pastor and congregation happens as an answer to prayer, the potential fruitfulness of this relationship is unlimited. Therefore, the first and greatest thing one can do in beginning a search for a pastorate is to make this enterprise a matter of continuing and prevailing prayer.

It is also important to keep in mind the necessity of patience. God's timing and His ways are not the same as ours, and so we often find ourselves having to wait for His provision. This can be exceedingly difficult when one has discovered "the hidden treasure" or "the pearl of great price" and is now willing to leave everything else behind in the quest to fulfill the holy calling from God. One naturally yearns to plunge ahead at full speed, but God does not always provide an immediate opportunity when one expects it, nor does He always open the kind of door that one has in mind. Just as the right spouse is worth the wait, the right ministry opportunity is worth the time spent in prayerful anticipation, and the appreciation of His gracious providence is increased in proportion to the patience that has been invested when a place of service has been secured. I well remember as a young man when I had recently surrendered to God's call to preach, how it seemed that the opportunities to preach were so far apart and that it seemed as though I would never be given a flock to feed! However, in God's perfect time the right opportunity came—actually it came within a little over a year after I surrendered to His call. I have never regretted the way He worked it all out, not only with my first pastorate but also with each successive one throughout the years.

In addition to prayer and patience, it is also necessary to make oneself available in a public kind of way. God uses people to accomplish His purposes, and He uses people to connect other people in potential relationships. Again, this can be quite similar to the way He provides a spouse. As for my wife and me, a pastor friend introduced us one Sunday night after the service when I visited his church, where she was a member. God could have arranged for us to meet some other way, but He used another person who knew us both to connect us together. He regularly does the same thing with ministers and churches. Most of human life comes down to relationships, and relationships are the vehicles God most often uses to connect His servants with ministry opportunities. Here are a few practical suggestions along this line. First, in addition to the public announcement of God's call in your life to your church and going through such things as being licensed into the Gospel ministry, be sure to let all your friends and acquaintances know you are available to be the pastor of a church. Along the way, friends from college or seminary as well as former professors from those days often can connect you with a potential opportunity. This also suggests the importance of staying connected with friends from prior associations, such as during college and seminary. Certainly someone you know will be aware of a potential pastorate for you; however, not all churches without pastors will be a potentially good ministry fit for you. It is also important that you cultivate relationships with other people in the ministry, particularly pastors. Networking with them is one of the best ways to find out about possible opportunities to serve. Also, it is highly advisable to form acquaintances with denominational leaders particularly at the local level but also beyond if you have the opportunity. These persons can help immensely, not only in discovering potential pastorates but also in screening them once a particular church has piqued your interest.

Being Baptist, one thing I have learned to do is always to connect with the local Director of Missions in the Baptist association to which a particular church I'm interested belongs. This person has always proven helpful to me in providing information about particular congregations. By arranging for a meeting with such a person face-to-face, he or she will be able to get a sense of you and what available churches might be a good fit for you. I'm sure other denominations have similar people at the local level that can be helpful in similar ways. These denominational workers sincerely want their local churches to do well, to have good pastors, and to have productive ministries in their communities, so these people have every reason to be motivated to help you find a place to serve. After you become a local pastor these denominational representatives continue to be valuable resource persons in all kinds of ways as you build a long-term ministry there. If you have a particular geographical area or region where you feel God leading you to serve, it is an extremely worthwhile investment to take a day, or even a week, and set up appointments with as many local denominational representatives in that region as possible, and then go sit down with them, giving them copies of your resume and talking with them about your sense of God's call and potential opportunities that might be available.

Another helpful thing is to make yourself available for pulpit supply as soon as you have been licensed by your church into the Gospel ministry. Here again, the local denominational representative (the associational Director of Missions if you are Baptist) can be instrumental in connecting you with churches that need someone to come and preach on a particular Sunday. On the one hand, a church may ask you to come and preach one Sunday, due to their pastor being sick, or perhaps he is away that weekend—in which case you will need to be sure to have a sermon ready for such an unforeseen opportunity. On the other hand, a church whose pastor has just moved on to another pastorate may need someone to fill the pulpit one or more Sundays as they make their plans as to how they will proceed during the interim period until they secure either an interim pastor or their next full-time pastor. You never know—a single engagement to preach to a particular congregation can open the door to all kinds of opportunities down the road, both with that local church and beyond. One of the most obvious clues that this may be happening is that perhaps you preach and the Lord really uses you in that congregation, so they ask you to come back the next week. If this happens a few more times, their Search Committee might ask you to be their interim pastor to lead the church and provide stability and ministry until they secure their next full-time pastor. Three of my eight pastorates began exactly this way! With the church that later became my first pastorate, I was asked to come and preach one Sunday a couple of weeks after their previous pastor had left. Soon after I went and preached, they asked me to come and do it again, so I did. After about the fourth time, their Search Committee sat down with me and asked me to be their interim pastor until they found their next full-time pastor, and I agreed. Over the next few months it became obvious that the Lord was at work through my efforts in the church, and after about six months He had worked it out that I became the full-time pastor! At the time, I had no education beyond high school, but the arrangement was worked out between me and the congregation that I could enroll in college and commute back and forth to school and also serve the church. Later, the same thing was worked out when I began seminary. Good thing I was young! Two other times over the years, I was between pastorates and preached as a "fill-in" one Sunday, which followed much the same course, leading to me becoming pastor of two other fine churches. This is just one of the many ways He can open doors for us. One clue that the Lord may be opening a door for you to become the pastor of a particular congregation, whether you are serving during the interim period on a temporary basis or if you have been contacted by their Search Committee and are going through the process that way—consider whether or not you get a sense that they *need you.* God usually brings a pastor to a particular congregation because that pastor has the right gifts and abilities to fit the needs of that flock. If you get a sense that you are needed by that church it is a really good sign.

There are also many other ways to make yourself known to congregations who are seeking pastors. Most seminaries and divinity schools are quite helpful to their students and alumni who are seeking ministry opportunities and can often connect you with a prospective congregation. Also there are websites, some connected with denominational agencies, while others are independently operated for the purpose of helping churches and ministers get together. All of these are legitimate and practical approaches, and you might want to try several different avenues as you seek to obey His call. Be patient, and the Lord will give you clear guidance in due time. Remember, the "Lord's hand is not shortened" (Is. 59:1), and there are no limits to the ways He can work. He can open a door which no one can shut (Rev. 3:7). To anyone who is truly called to a life of ministry, my best advice would be to make yourself available, and God will surely provide an opportunity.

Chapter 6

Laying the Foundation:
Getting Off to a Good Start

"Therefore whosoever heareth these sayings of mine, and doeth them, I will liken him unto a wise man, which built his house upon a rock" (Matt. 7:24).

My father was a carpenter for many years, and my first job during high school and for 12 years afterward was working with him as a carpenter. During the first few years I failed to really appreciate all I was learning, but as boyhood gave way to manhood and even more in the years that followed I came to realize more and more the value of the knowledge and skills that I gained, not to mention the time spent with my wonderful father, who is now gone from the earth. One of the most important things I learned from him during the building of the 44 houses he and I built together—one at a time, just the two of us—was the importance of the foundation and getting everything started off right. If you think about it, everything in building a house depends in large part upon how you get started. If the foundation is not quite level, then the whole house will be on a slant, and you'll be in big trouble when you start hanging doors, which either won't stay closed or won't stay open, not to mention a host of other problems that will occur. If it is not laid out square, you'll have all kinds of problems trying to get plywood (which is square) for the subflooring and sheetrock (which is also square) for the walls and ceilings to fit together correctly. Furthermore, if the foundation is not strong enough to carry the weight of the structure, then what you're building can never last very long or be worth very much. It all depends upon the foundation and how you get started.

For a pastor, the same principle applies: How you get started will have a great bearing on the quality and longevity of the ministry you are building with a particular congregation. Take your time, think ahead, and be careful! Starting out is important work, and being deliberate at this stage is an investment that can bring great dividends in the future. Unlike a building, where your materials are produced to industry standards with regard to such things as size and strength and there are uniform codes to govern the process, with building a ministry you are working with the stuff of relationships as you interact with people, no two of whom are exactly alike. Recognizing also that no two pastors or congregations are just alike either, here are a few general suggestions which may prove helpful.

First, invest a generous amount of time and energy getting to know your congregation and its history. Just as if you have stepped into a flowing river there is upstream water which has not yet arrived which represents the future and there is downstream water much of which has already disappeared which represents the past. Here you are at this particular point where you can see some of what is ahead and some of what has happened but much in either direction is beyond your view. As you look more carefully you notice an uprooted tree which has been brought down by the current and is caught in some rocks just below you, giving you a valuable clue along with a line of smaller debris a few feet up the bank along each side that indicates there must have been a major storm in the not too distant past which temporarily caused the river to overflow and may have even altered its course somewhat. The more you investigate the more you learn about this river—and about this congregation into whose moving waters you have now stepped. Take the time to learn about the flow of this church in the past—it can help you to anticipate what to expect in the future in many ways. Has there been a major "storm" that these fine people have weathered recently, and what was it like? Have there been major conflicts in recent years? What were they about? Were they really ever settled? Were there winners and losers? Did everyone stay, or did some leave, and if so where did they go? Or have there been other traumas, tragedies, or perhaps victories and celebrations that have affected the course of the church? All these things take time to find out, and as you investigate you will almost certainly discover that different people in the church remember these things quite differently from one another. It is a puzzle you must piece together over time as you get to know the people. As with the Biblical picture of a shepherd and flock you must invest the time and energy forming relationships among your congregation in order to build the necessary trust they must have in you to let you lead. You may have been voted in as pastor by a unanimous ballot, but you will never really *become* their shepherd until they know in their hearts that you really love Jesus, that you are truly reliable, and that you absolutely care for them. This will take time.

It sounds like a daunting task, but it does not really have to be. Let's say you've just moved into the church parsonage (every pastor should experience living in a parsonage at least once!), and it's your first weekday in the office. What should you do? Where will you start? To be realistic, there is probably already a mountain of work which you will have to do right away—perhaps hospital calls, committee meetings, staff situations to address, or an unexpected death of a church member for which you must now plan a funeral, etc. Again, you've stepped into an ever-flowing stream, and the stuff of human life and death is on going. The jump rope is turning, and you must "run in" and start! When you do get a free hour or two, however, take a stroll through the church cemetery, if there is one. You can learn a great deal about a church as you compare the family names in the most recent directory with the names on the tombstones. You can find out who the prominent families in the church have been (and maybe still are), and you can also perhaps learn of past hurts for which there is still need of healing. I vividly remember when we had just come to our second church that I noticed in the cemetery a line of gravestones, all of one family. Six little children who all died at different times within about a five year period before any of them reached adolescence, then a mother who died in her thirties, a father who lived to be almost eighty, a second wife, and a third wife who also preceded him in death. So much grief in this family! I inquired about this and learned that there had been several winters of severe influenza during that time, and that all those children died of it, along with the mother. I also learned that one daughter had survived, and she was still alive and well, though no longer in our church and in her sixties at that time. I learned that the father had been an active member and leader in the church and community throughout his life, and that there were still some relatives in the congregation.

Another valuable tool for learning the story of your church is the Minute Book, which contains the records of your church's business meetings. This is especially valuable if your church is congregational in polity, which means most matters of importance are decided by a vote of the congregation. Take the time to read through it, at least the records for the past several years, and you will learn a great deal about what has gone on. You will also learn who the real "movers and shakers" have been, who introduced business or who held things up or otherwise wielded power. You may be surprised or perhaps shocked at what you learn, but you *need to know*. You will also get a window on what the issues and problems in the fellowship may have been as well as some that perhaps are still ongoing, depending on how detailed the minutes are. You need to know these things in order to avoid "stepping into a hole." Another important document that will often give you a window on the church's history is the Constitution and By-Laws. Give special attention to any amendments, for they often are introduced as a result of issues or problems which have come up. A third source, which will help you get a sense of the church's values and priorities, is the annual church budget. This will lay out for you what the church considers to be more and less important from a financial standpoint, which usually turns out to be quite reliable as an indicator. A little research in documents such as these will be well worth your time and may spare you a good deal of grief.

There will also be much more that you will just have to use your eyes and ears to learn, which will take time. In another congregation that I served years ago, a wife and mother in a prominent family obviously carried a heavy load of anger and resentment, and this made it hard for most people to be around her. She also seemed to especially take a disliking to me, almost from the start.

Over the first few years of my pastorate there, it seemed that she and I happened to clash every time I tried to initiate anything new or to show leadership in the church in any way. As a result, her husband and other family members also were drawn in on her side many times. In about my fifth year there, I found out why: When this middle-aged woman had been a nine or ten-year-old girl, her mother had gone into the hospital to give birth to a new baby. (This was before the days of ultrasound or many other technologies in common use today.) It turned out that instead of being pregnant, her mother had a football sized tumor that had to be removed from her abdomen, and she never survived to come home from the hospital. Imagine this young girl's emotional trauma when one of the happiest occasions—the birth of a baby—gave way to the saddest of experiences—the death of her mother! No wonder she was mad at the world, and especially at God, whom I the pastor represented. I would like to say that I was able to help her deal with her feelings and move beyond her pain. Unfortunately, I'm afraid too much had already happened for me to be one to whom she would respond. However, I learned some valuable lessons from this difficult situation. It also helped me be more compassionate toward her, now that I knew her story. Everything makes more sense when you know the story.

As suggested by the account given above, every church member has a story that often provides the key to ministry for that person. Likewise, every congregation of believers has its own story which will largely give you a picture of the experiences, choices, victories, and failures which have shaped this flock, giving you the under-shepherd the necessary clues for making a ministry diagnosis in order to help this church move forward in a Kingdom direction. At the same time, it is important to realize that sometimes there will be situations that you either misread or cannot know about, and there are people who, try as you might, may never regard you as *their* pastor. It may be that something as minor as your looks, manner, or even the sound of your voice evokes a negative response from them. You may bring back a memory of someone else with whom he or she has had a negative experience in the past. There will likely be a few people with whom you may never be able to overcome this, but over time as you continue to prayerfully show patience and compassion you will usually be able to win them over. With difficult people it often comes down to your being there and responding to their needs when a crisis comes, as it eventually will for us all. Again, all of this takes time, and as mentioned before, ministry is much like farming—it involves planting, cultivating, waiting, praying—and *time*—before the harvest. Take the time to listen, to observe, to reflect and consider. Beware of "pulling up the wheat with the tares" by moving slowly and carefully with regard to initiating changes, especially during the first couple of years until you've laid a strong foundation of relationships. Out of this groundwork, trust in your leadership can develop which will support long-term cooperative ministry with pastor and church together serving the larger community and our Lord.

Having invested yourself in learning the individual stories and the corporate story of your flock, and having begun the formation of loving, trusting relationships with them, you will soon have a fertile seedbed for developing a realistic ministry vision and strategy together under the guidance of

the Holy Spirit. Not only are you getting to know them—
they are getting to know *you*. As you demonstrate that you
truly care for them and that you can be relied upon to do
your best, they will come to trust you and be willing to
follow your leadership as you begin to try to move the
flock forward. As you "keep watch" over your flock, you
will notice not only who the leaders and power people in
the church are, you will also begin to get a picture of who
the *reliable* people are, who follow through with tasks and
are faithful in the overall life of the flock and are team
players. You will also pick up on who the people are who
communicate, either in verbal or nonverbal ways, that they
consider themselves *entitled* to positions of leadership,
perhaps because of their family history in the church or
because of their giftedness. Incidentally, the most gifted
people are not always the most reliable and faithful people
when entrusted with much responsibility. In fact, often an
extremely gifted person turns out to be much less reliable
and effective in leadership because they do not have to
work very hard at what they do. For example, the best
musician in the church is often not the best person to lead
the choir. I would much rather have a person leading the
music who can bring the choir together to work as a team,
even if that person doesn't know music as well as someone
else. Remember also, that humility, rather than pride, gives
evidence of a willingness to learn and be led by the Holy
Spirit. You will probably also find, that those who consider
themselves entitled are some of the very ones who occupy
the positions of leadership when you get there. Sometimes
these people "come around" over time, but more often they
will have their own agenda that is usually tied to the status
quo. Prayerfully give yourself and them some time: it is
amazing how the Holy Spirit can work when He is given

time and space. Remember, we are called to a work we cannot do, but *He can!* In the first couple of years, it is wise to invest a large part of your time observing and listening, as you carefully lay the foundation for your work with these people in the years to come. Too often, what should have been fruitful pastorates are aborted because the pastor came in with an agenda to remake the congregation "after his own image and likeness" and did not take the time or expend the energy to get to know the people and find out what the long-term opportunities and capabilities were really likely to be. Only in taking the time to lay a good foundation by getting to know the people and building strong, trusting and loving relationships, can you then develop a realistic vision for what you and your flock will be able to do together in the years to come. We will talk more about this in the next chapter, but the development of a vision and helping it take root in your congregation, along with identifying those whom He would have to be leaders, is one of the greatest factors relating to the fruitfulness of your time spent together as shepherd and flock over the years and generations to come.

Chapter 7

Love Them Into the Kingdom: Maximizing Your Ministry

As we have already indicated, ministry happens in the context of relationships if it is to happen at all. The Biblical picture of shepherd and sheep is the paradigm for leading a church, with the under-shepherd or pastor and his flock. This concept can only be fully appreciated when one recognizes the work involved for one who would lead a flock or congregation as primarily that of building relationships where the bonds of mutual love and trust are continually strengthened over time as life in Christ is experienced together.

As with the shepherd of actual sheep, the pastor of a local congregation of believers is entrusted with multiple responsibilities, which include such things as building trust between the individual members of the flock and the shepherd, maintaining peace between those individuals and each other and fostering their mutual oneness as members of the same flock or congregation. The shepherd cannot really begin to lead the flock until the members *see themselves* as belonging together. (To mix metaphors, cowboys do not start a cattle drive until there has first been a roundup!) There is a big difference between a bunch of sheep and a flock, and there is likewise a huge difference between a crowd of people and a congregation. They must see themselves as belonging together, and that means relationships among the members must be made and kept strong by their mutual fulfillment in loving relationships with one another *and with their shepherd.* As pastor, your role as a relationship builder is a major key to the wellbeing and health of the flock with which you are entrusted. Just as the owner of a flock of sheep entrusts their care to a shepherd, who leads, feeds, and cares for the various needs of his flock, the Chief Shepherd, Jesus Christ, has entrusted to you and to me the care of His flock, and we are accountable to Him for the quality of our work, which is primarily relational. As we are faithful in this work, our Master can be counted on to add new sheep to the flock, and they will need to be intentionally included in the relational network of the congregation as a whole. Assuming from the previous chapter that you have begun your work with the congregation the Lord has provided for you and have begun laying the relational foundation by learning as much as you can of their story, let's consider a few facets of your task in moving the flock to "green pastures." Here we will try to focus on principles, rather than prescribing a list of "simple steps," since each pastor and congregation is different, with different stories, gifts, opportunities, and challenges.

Woven into the warp and woof of leadership is the reality of guiding your congregation through change. There is no avoiding change. (I'm confronted with it every time I look into the mirror!) The real choice is whether we deal with it in a proactive or reactive manner. Over my years in pastoral ministry, perhaps one of the most exasperating situations that I've faced in several congregations has been the severity of resistance to change that permeates many churches. We claim to believe a Gospel of transformation—change—but in practice we often deny that truth by trying to keep everything the same. What this really comes down to is that living by faith does not come naturally to us at all—it's a supernatural, miraculous kind of life that only God through His Spirit can produce in His body the Church! Our natural inclination is to stay within the security of our comfort zone in areas that seem safe because they are familiar. Living by faith requires us to risk the unknown as we follow our Shepherd, relying upon His direction and provision rather than going our own way. Therefore, as the under-shepherd, who goes in front of his flock, it is crucial that you model for your flock a close walk with Him, the Chief Shepherd. Just as your automobile has several gauges on the dash panel to indicate the running condition of your vehicle, there are several "gauges" which indicate the spiritual health of an individual or a congregation. One of the most important of these is our willingness to face change. Certainly it should not need to be said that there are certain tenets of the our message which are timeless and unchangeable, but how we relate our faith to a changing culture says a great deal about where we are in our walk with God. I've said all this to make one point: If you want your congregation to be open to change, you yourself must demonstrate that you are adaptable as well. In fact, you may have to try several approaches in introducing change in your congregation before you get it just right! Praise the Lord for first pastorates, where we "cut our teeth" by not getting it right the first time! I said something like this earlier, but it bears repeating, "I'm sure there's a special place in heaven for *my* first church!" Actually, for me at least, all of the eight congregations I have served have been learning experiences, though at least after the first one I did for the most part know the ABC's!

How and when a particular change is introduced has a great deal to do with how it will be perceived. When you first come on the scene as the new pastor, most congregations will "extend you a line of credit" with regard to your doing some things differently than "Rev. Jones." Be careful, especially at first, about introducing major changes that can possibly be put off—you don't want to "overdraw" on your "credit line!" If you do, you may not have enough "collateral" down the road when a more crucial change needs to be made. When you do initiate a change, it is wise to begin with something that will be both *painless and productive for them.* Not really knowing you, they need to see immediate benefit that does not cost them, in order that you will appear in their minds as wise, competent, and trustworthy *from the start.* Then as time passes, and they know you more intimately as you have conducted yourself consistently, they will learn to trust you more fully. Consider also that what seems minor to you may be major to them. Do some informal polling among the members you know the best before introducing something unfamiliar to the congregation. When you're new, you'll probably need to rely upon members of the Search Committee who brought you to the church—they have a vested interest in your being successful. Hopefully, the members of this committee represent a cross section of the church, but you can't always count on it. Over time, you will learn whom to trust. Here again, it comes down to relationships, and relationships are built by loving communication—over time.

Once you've invested yourself in laying an adequate foundation in your first couple of years with your church, you should have a pretty clear general picture of the spiritual condition of your congregation as a whole, as well as their strengths and weaknesses, gifts and needs. You should also by now have identified for the most part who the real leaders are—they're not always the people in the most prominent positions, as we've already noted. Down the road, others will surprise and thrill you by emerging as responsible leaders as your church's ministry develops and blossoms. Also as previously mentioned, you will by now have begun to spot some people who for whatever reason are not reliable in following through when given responsibility, or are slaves to their own agendas or the status quo, which is keeping them from being team players who work well with others toward common goals. Even more importantly, the Holy Spirit should be formulating in your mind a vision for what the needs are in your larger community and what the resources available to your congregation are for meeting those needs. These two factors—needs and resources—will become the framework for you and your flock's ministry life together, and these two factors will help shape the development of a ministry plan or strategy for your congregation. Back to the needs and shortcomings of your congregation—which everyone has: these miraculously tend to be addressed and overcome in the process of ministry to the outside community! Like Andrew (John 6:8-9), who took inventory after being faced with feeding the hungry multitude and discovered a boy who had brought his lunch, we often discover that we really do have *something* our Lord can use in meeting the need. As that story ends, the point is made that there were twelve baskets of food left over—more than they started with— and there were *twelve* disciples. It seems clear that their needs were met through being involved in ministry! Often, the real challenge is to get our congregations to turn their focus outward, rather than focusing on their own traditions and comfort. It is a shame that so many churches (and pastors) have no long-term ministry plan. For some congregations their future plans extend no further than to "come back next Sunday." Likewise, the only document they have that reflects any kind of thinking ahead is the annual church budget—on which they simply adjusted the figures from the year before, which indicates that they're not planning on doing anything different. No wonder so many churches and pastors are struggling and frustrated! Now let's look at two contrasting examples of ministry situations.

In one of the churches I served, following the first Sunday evening service that I led, when I went to the front door to greet the people as they left I discovered it was locked—everyone used the side door on Sunday evenings. The next week I pointed out that newcomers would try to enter by the front door, not knowing that we only use the side door at night, and I suggested that we start opening it. (Many churches have "private club" habits or traditions that they do not even realize hinder new people!) At least metaphorically if not literally, when we started opening the front door Jesus came right in—He'd probably been knocking awhile (Rev. 3:20)! During my seven-and-a-half years there the church almost tripled, and we had to build a new worship center, renovated the parsonage into offices, turned the old sanctuary into education space, remodeled an adjacent house into a children's center, and added paid staff. These things did not *just happen.* Early in my third year there I enlisted a group of people into a long-range planning committee, which we called "The Dream Team," and together we worked for nine months studying our church and community and "brought forth" a five year ministry plan which contained five kinds of goals: growth, new ministries, facilities, staff, and finances. You will have to follow the Spirit's guidance for yourself here, but I took the risk of personally choosing the five members of this team rather than working through some existing group like the deacons or church council. Again, some of the people in leadership positions were not the right people to have on such a project. Sure enough, I did get some "flak" from some who thought they were entitled to be included, but it was worth what it cost me for this team to have the right DNA. All the people I enlisted were long-time but forward thinking, faithful church members who were influential throughout the congregation. I didn't select any newer members, since those who were new were not tied to the church's past traditions and would already be open to change. The Dream Team and I formulated a written-out plan for the next five years that communicated the vision God had given me and which they had now caught. Then in a special church conference each member of the team shared one of the five parts with the congregation, and the church, which God was already blessing with new people, bought into the plan and adopted it. For the next few years it was the nearest thing to the first few chapters of The Book of Acts I have ever experienced! Of course Satan had perfect attendance and tried to interfere at every turn, but God was able to do much more than he was! When you have a vision and can get a few key people to catch a glimpse of it, own it, and together share it with the church so that the people buy into it, God can really do great things!

I must not conclude this chapter without saying that in all honesty not every situation is one in which the scenario described above will happen. You must be willing to "bloom where you are planted." I have been the pastor "just down the street" from the church that was exploding with growth more times than I've been in the one having all the excitement. A later pastorate than the one I just described was in a church that had been fraught with conflict and had forced the previous two pastors to leave, with the last one taking about a third of the congregation with him to start a new church a couple of miles away. Instead of this church experiencing great growth and "mighty things," I spent over eight years trying to stop the bleeding and help heal that broken body from which a third part had been crudely amputated. My ministry there for the most part became one of trying to help some of those people get beyond their pain and anger and to help others recognize that they weren't "the winners" because they were the ones still here with the building and bankroll. There were also many "agendas" at work that were fueled by the healthiest "gossip grapevine" I've ever seen anywhere I've been. This was a group of sheep that really knew very little about being a flock, though they thought the opposite was true. The whole time I was there it seemed that there was "a pot boiling over" all the time! During the "laying the foundation" phase of my time there, I really began to see and finally was brought face-to-face with the stark fact that the most I could hope for was to give them a few years of peace and stability on which perhaps the next pastor could then build. Because the dynamics that had caused the previous conflicts were still at work in an unhealthy body which clearly was not willing to make the drastic lifestyle changes necessary to become healthy, I was forced to aim much lower when formulating my long-term vision than I thought at the outset of my time there. It was also a vision which made my situation quite lonely, since I could not share it with the congregation for what I hope are obvious reasons—I was in a sick church that didn't want to think, much less be told, that they were a sick church. I was with a group of people who wanted the church to be bigger and have more money, but they were not willing to be led through the radical changes that would lead to health. Due to issues with previous pastors, they wanted the pastor to be a caregiver but not a leader. The commitment among the membership and even among many of the leaders (some of whom were paid) was extremely low. Why would anyone want to become vulnerable by fully investing in a body that has a history of so much pain? Over time, it became my first priority that when the time came I must "land the plane" safely so that everyone could get off in one piece, and hopefully most of the church would have the healthy experience of missing the last pastor instead of rejoicing that he was gone. If I was faithful in this, perhaps the stage would be set for the next pastor to actually be able to build. I cannot adequately describe the inner battle I repeatedly fought during those years as I struggled to bring peace and unity to a sick congregation I would never have considered joining if I had been someone in the community who was simply looking for a church to be part of. There were two things that kept me there for more than eight years: First, this was *the door* that God had opened and He repeatedly closed every other opportunity for me to fulfill His call to be a pastor, so I *knew* this was where He wanted me. (Remember, at times it is absolutely crucial to be sure of His call!) Secondly, I genuinely loved these hurting and angry people, and I realized that if I did not stay to help them God would have to send someone else to do what I was unwilling to do. I also considered that a medical doctor doesn't go to work at the hospital every day because he loves to be around sickness and death, but because he is needed—even when the sickness may be contagious or terminal. I knew they *needed* me, so I stayed until I was sure I could do no more. Looking back, I am certain I could not have completed this pastorate in a positive way had I been a younger, less experienced man. Thank God! He always knows what He is doing, though I often do not know what He is doing—or even what I am doing!

Of the two examples from my own pastorates I have shared above, I hope you can appreciate which one would have been the most difficult. Also the fact that the exciting experience had already happened made the difficult one all the harder, since I knew how it *could* be! On the other hand, only God knows in which situation the most abiding fruit will have been borne, and each was valuable in shaping me as a Christian and as a pastor. It also bears mentioning as I hinted above that as a pastor I view myself as a link in a chain. I must consider that someone else, perhaps quite different in gifts, personality, and perspective, will be the next pastor. It is incumbent upon me that when the time comes, I leave things better than I found them, and hopefully by God's grace I will have helped the next pastor be in a position to lead the church on to a higher level than I was able to do. It is also as true today as it was with Israel in The Book of Numbers: Sometimes congregations make choices that put many of the blessings of God on hold until another generation comes along. It is a sad fact, that Pastor Search

Committees do not always tell you (nor do they sometimes even know) what the real condition of their congregation is. (Remember, every family seems "normal" to those who are part of it.) You really cannot grasp their full condition until you've been there awhile. Then with God's help you can know and do what He sent you there to do, which may prove to be quite different than you thought at first. Your job is to love the people and be faithful to His call. He who parted the Red Sea can be trusted to provide a way for you wherever He leads.

Chapter 8

Don't Strike the Rock! Dealing with Opposition

There are a couple of Old Testament stories about God providing water from a rock for the children of Israel through Moses that are quite similar but have a stark contrast. The first is in Exodus 17, soon after the Red Sea crossing before they reached Sinai and received The Law. Israel was complaining for lack of water, and God instructed Moses to strike a particular rock with the rod which had signaled all the plagues against Egypt and water came forth. The second story takes place many years later and is located shortly after the death of Miriam in Numbers 20, near the conclusion of a section in the book which began in chapter thirteen that records repeated "murmurings" in the wilderness by Israel against Moses and against God. Here, Moses is instructed to *speak* to the rock in the presence of the congregation with the promise that water would come forth to quench their thirst. However, instead of speaking to the rock, Moses strikes it as before—he actually strikes it twice—and calls the people rebels. (I've wondered if he struck the rock because he felt like taking a swing at a few of those people!) The water still comes forth as God meets the nation's need, but God reprimands Moses and Aaron for unbelief and for not sanctifying or honoring God in the eyes of the people. They are forbidden to enter Canaan. Whatever else was going on in the latter story, one thing is clear: Moses lost his cool! I'm sure that all the murmurings recorded in the preceding chapters had taken their collective toll until he reached the breaking point and expressed his anger at the wrong time and in the wrong way. Forty years of his life had been invested in this trip, and now he could no longer hope to enter the Promised Land! What a price to pay!

Without launching forth into the depths of Old Testament Theology and how it relates to New Testament Theology, suffice it to say that the Old Testament by and large (particularly the Torah) emphasizes the holiness of God, though grace is present, while the New Testament emphasizes His grace, though holiness is still evident. Due to His divine genius, God's holiness revealed through the Law was presented first to show us our need of His grace, made available through Christ. I am so very glad that in Christ every sin has been covered, and God's grace is always sufficient. Having said all this, it is still important to remember that His grace does not abrogate the principles of sowing and reaping, and in this life we must still deal with the ramifications of our choices. Moses' temper got the best of him in a public way and compromised his ability to represent God and to lead effectively. It is important that we who lead God's people today do not miss the valuable lesson to be learned here. The Book of Numbers records numerous conflict situations, particularly from chapter thirteen up to chapter twenty, as the Israelites refused to follow God through Moses' leadership into Canaan, as various groups and individuals—even Aaron and Miriam— challenged his fitness to lead. It must have seemed to Moses that everyone was against him. Sadly, it is apparent that he didn't always channel his anger very well— Confession time! I too have encountered opposition and downright defiance among those God sent me to lead, and I have been angered by it. To get it all out, I also sometimes have trouble channeling my anger. Every once in a while I encounter someone in the congregation who knows how to "push all my buttons" in just the right sequence to set me ablaze if I'm not careful. A few times I've not been very careful—and it has cost me, perhaps more than I know. I will say, however, that I have never *completely* lost control, though I know of a few occasions where "my stovepipe glowed red" from the fire in my furnace! I should never have allowed even that to show! One of my closest pastor friends' has a saying: "We all pay for our education." Well, in this course I received no scholarship but have paid the full tuition! That said, I have also learned a few things along the way.

Contrary to what some people seem to think, anger in and of itself is not necessarily wrong. After all, Jesus was angry in the synagogue (Mark 3:5), and I am sure that when He cleared the outer court of the Jerusalem temple during Holy Week, He was not exactly pleased with the commerce that had been substituted for worship, either. Doubtless, there are things that really should anger us—injustice, mistreatment of children or the abuse or oppression of other helpless people, to mention just a few. However, like a fire, anger can easily burn out of control and become destructive in all kinds of ways. James tells us "the wrath of man worketh not the righteousness of God" (James 1:20). When I think about it, any time I respond to another person in anger, even by just raising my voice or giving a sullen or disdainful look, the version of me—no, the version of *Jesus* that people see—is not the version of Him that they should be seeing at that moment.

So the question arises, "Does that mean I cannot be angry?" Not at all! In fact, the ability to feel anger is part of what it is to be a human being, created in the image of God—who also is Himself sometimes angry. The answer is that anger must be handled carefully and channeled properly. While anger makes for a great fire in the boiler to power the locomotive, it makes for a poor engineer who will fail to slow down for the curve and will wreck the whole train. Anger at injustice, abuse, racism, or a myriad of other evils can help motivate us to take strong and needful stands on important moral and spiritual issues; however, we must be controlled not by anger but by love, which God has "shed abroad in our hearts by the Holy Spirit" (Romans 5:5). What people need to see from us is not our wrath but our compassion for those victimized. When we are personally opposed, persecuted, misrepresented, slandered and ridiculed as ministers of the Gospel, what an opportunity we have for cheek turning and showing the most powerful side of Jesus that people can ever see! It is only through the Holy Spirit at work in our lives that this will happen. It is *not* our natural, human inclination. To be honest, the times I responded in anger when I have been opposed in churches were also times when my prayer life and my walk with Jesus was not what it should have been. In truth, those were times when my focus was on *myself* and how *I* was being treated. Only when we are surrendered to the control of the Holy Spirit, can we "be angry and sin not" (Ephesians 4:26) and also let go of that anger before it solidifies into resentment and then hardens into bitterness. God the Holy Spirit, who lives within us, can enable us to do that which we cannot—return good for evil, which is the only way evil can be overcome (Romans 12:21).

So then, how do we deal with opposition, particularly when people defy our leadership and try their best to thwart us as we try to shepherd His flock? First, pray—a lot! It seems like Moses was "on his face" most of the time in Exodus and Numbers. (Unfortunately, I guess there was one time he forgot!) If we stay "on our faces" it will keep us humble, and it will also keep our focus on Him and not on ourselves. If our focus is really on Him, then by His Spirit we will respond as He would respond. What is more, if we sincerely pray for those who oppose us and "bless them" (pronounce the blessings of God upon them) as Jesus instructed us in Matthew 5:44, we will have chosen in our hearts to respond in love, and it will help us to forgive and let go. Second, we need to be sure that we really *listen* to those who seem to oppose us. Another of my pastor friends has said many times, "We pastors tend to be overbearing." Sadly, he's right! We preach and teach and lead, and we're called of God to do this. It's easy to get caught up in what we're doing and forget that we don't have a corner on the truth or on how things should be done. There is also an outside chance that we may have missed something—the person opposing us may have a valid reason for seeing things differently. We won't know if we don't listen to them. Moreover, no one likes to be brushed aside. If we do this to the same person more than a very few times, we run the risk of losing any future opportunity to work with that person or to influence them in a Kingdom way. Likewise, if we allow this to become a habit and if others continually see us discounting the value of another person's opinions, they will soon begin to lose respect for us and our ability to lead.

On the other hand, it is much better to try to create a team atmosphere in the church and to include everyone we possibly can in some capacity. In football, the quarterback does not carry the ball on every play. Instead, he hands it off or throws a pass to another player regularly, which gives him a break and at the same time allows others to use their abilities. There are also many players on the team who never touch the ball, but their roles are also important for moving it forward. It may be that the person who opposes you could also fill a spot on your team if you try to include him or her. That doesn't mean you have to let him or her carry the ball, at least to start with, but if you can involve that person at some level you have turned a negative into a positive and you may have turned a potential adversary into a friend. Another advantage of taking a team approach to ministry is that other members of your team may be able to play a mediating role in helping you relate to that person or persons who oppose you. It may be that they can reach out and include those who oppose if they won't respond to you alone. Also, it never hurts for those you trust to know something of your struggle and your desire to include those hard-to-reach people, so they'll know how to pray for you. Having said this, it is a fact that here and there you will encounter a few people who will oppose you to the bitter end, no matter what, and you will never be able to win them over, no matter what you do. However, it is important that you still try—even when you are convinced that there is no hope. After all, God still loves them, so we cannot give up either. That doesn't mean you have to bring them flowers or shower them with gifts. (You might want to try that if nothing else works!) The rest of your flock also needs to see that you are willing to go to great lengths to be a compassionate shepherd, and they will see it most clearly when they see your patient forbearance and attempts to win over those who openly resist your leadership. It really shouldn't surprise us when we are opposed, since leadership is all about introducing your flock to new areas of pasture which are different than they've experienced before—it's about introducing change. Finally, cultivate some close friendships with other pastors. (A later chapter includes more about this.) Some of my most treasured friendships are with pastor friends that go back to our college and seminary days. Others are with fellow pastors He brought into my life in various other ways. Shepherding God's flock can be lonely work, and the fact is, no one but another shepherd really knows what it is like. As stated earlier, being a shepherd is one thing, and being one of the sheep is in many ways quite different. There will be struggles you face that only one who has walked where you walk will understand. There will be other struggles that only the Great Shepherd Himself will fully understand. Keep these relationships strong!

I am sure that the picture of Moses striking the rock and calling the people a bunch of rebels would have been a mental image most of the Israelites would have found difficult to forget. If we respond in anger to our adversaries we hand them a weapon to use against us—a not so pretty picture that people will find hard to forget. Thankfully, the One who indwells us is always available to help if we will but seek Him, and He will enable us to respond as our Lord Jesus would respond if we will only remember to seek Him.

Chapter 9

Where the Stumps Are:
Potentially Hazardous Zones

In most large lakes, in dangerous shallow areas where unseen rocks or stumps lurk below the surface, there are usually marker buoys located nearby to alert boaters of the unseen hazards. Unfortunately, there are sometimes areas that perhaps should be marked but are not, for whatever reason. You just have to know they are there, and if you don't know their location you "learn" where they are by "finding" them, perhaps bending a boat propeller in the process or worse. The safest way to learn about these dangerous places is to have them pointed out to you by someone else who either "found" them or was also warned, which spares you the risk of damage to your boat and may well save your life. Likewise, in leading a flock of believers, there can be areas into which you should move cautiously and never approach at full speed. Certainly there are a few almost universally known dangers that every pastor should avoid, such as getting into potentially compromising situations with persons of the opposite sex. Paul's admonition, "Abstain from all appearance of evil" (I Thess. 5:22) is a prudent motto for our day in this regard. It is a sad fact that in today's culture just an accusation along this line is enough to brand you for life, so be careful. Our purpose here is to help prepare you to spot some of the less obvious hazards, before you "run aground." Some of these and other potential dangers may be somehow marked, as you find documentation of a prior church problem in the church's business meeting Minute Book, for example. However, there will almost always be other, maybe even more dangerous areas that you either just "encounter" and pay the consequences, or hopefully someone warns you about. Shepherding a congregation also carries with it the reality that every day is a new experience in which situations can and do arise which you had not expected. In churches there occur unexpected sicknesses, tragedies, deaths, or community situations, such as perhaps even the rerouting of a street or highway that can suddenly and drastically alter the day-to-day flow of the life in your flock in ways you never anticipated. Take it for granted that you will occasionally be taken off guard, and you will not always respond perfectly in every situation that comes up. This is really just part of the "stuff of life" through which we all learn and grow. At the same time, many things that come up are things for which you can prepare, at least partially, in advance. For example, let's say you're fresh out from seminary with a divinity degree, a shiny new Bible, and you've just moved to your first church. You're all set! Right? Well, maybe but perhaps not. Let's suppose that the day you move into the parsonage you get a call from the local funeral home that Mrs. Smith, a prominent member of your church died last night, and they are calling on behalf of the family to discuss the lady's funeral. Will you be ready? It depends on several things, but much has to do with whether or not you have already considered what is involved in planning and conducting a funeral. If you have looked ahead, for example, by securing a Minister's Manual or a copy of *The Book of Common Prayer,* you will at least have in your library some resources that can give you guidance in the process.   While you cannot be completely ready for most things before they occur, there are certain things, like deaths, which are going to happen and you will have to deal with, ready or not.   The thrust of this chapter is simply this: prepare for what you know is coming, and don't step into unnecessary difficulties.   Following the counsel given previously in the chapter "Laying the Foundation" will greatly help you in the years that follow to avoid many of the pitfalls in leading your flock. The more you learn about your people and their story, the more likely you will be able to identify areas in your ministry there where you will need to be careful. Having said all this, let's take a look at some common things to watch out for.

Introduce Change Carefully

As I've already stated, being the shepherd of a flock means you are in the business of leading them forward to "green pastures," which involves leading them through change. Though I've talked at length about introducing change in a couple of previous chapters, it is such a central facet of your work, carrying with it so many potential hazards, that it merits reinforcement from this perspective, though I hope to not be too redundant.

The first bit of advice, which I reemphasize here, is to avoid changing too much too soon. How much is too much and how soon is too soon is something you and the Lord will have to clarify between yourselves, but here are a few general guidelines. At the outset, let me say that when I began each of the eight pastorates with which I have thusfar been entrusted, almost immediately I saw things I wanted to change. Some of these things I was able to get handled fairly soon, and others were still the way they were the day I arrived on the day I left. And quite likely they continue as they were to this day. This brings up a somewhat unpleasant thought—just because I want something to be changed that does not necessarily mean it *should* be changed. Moreover, just because something needs to be changed, that does not necessarily mean that it *can* be changed, at least not without causing harm in the church. More than once, there were changes I thought were of critical importance early on, but over time realized that there were other more pressing needs to be addressed than those. Be aware, your priorities may need some adjustment as you get to know your congregation.

Go slow with major changes even after you've grown familiar with your people, unless you have absolutely clear direction from God and *unless you are willing to pay whatever it might cost you.* If you proceed cautiously, you may be able to assess both the potential good a particular change may bring, as well as any negative effects that may come up down the road. As was mentioned earlier, if a change you initiate turns out to be more negative than positive *in the minds of your people,* you are likely to lose some of your "collateral" with them for enacting other changes in the future. Don't forget they are volunteers, so be sure to do your best to figure *their cost* into the equation ahead of time. Again, remember the saying, "Not every hill is a hill to die on"! Some, more minor changes, especially those that are important *but will also be painless* for the flock, may be fairly safe to go ahead and implement, if you follow the proper channels for whatever it involves. It may take you some time to find out what those channels are and to get approval. Remember, in many churches not everything will always be clearly defined as part of some leader or committee's job description. Often many of the process rules can be unwritten but assumed that "everyone knows." A church where this is the case is usually a congregation that is not accustomed to much change, so your work may be cut out for you. Whatever it takes, do whatever you can to follow the existing process, whether it's clearly defined or not. That way, when you've gotten approval, you then have some companions "out on the limb" with you! Some things, like my suggesting that we start unlocking the front door of the sanctuary for Sunday night worship, mentioned earlier, don't really require any action to make and are just common sense. Things like that are generally pretty safe. On the other hand, if you want to move the nursery into the parlor that has a plaque over the door that says, "Aunt Ruth's Parlor: Her Furniture, Doilies, and Bible Donated by her Children," I would say, "Steer clear!" In fact, if that proposal ever comes up I would make sure to be sitting on the other side of the building from whoever brings that up! You'd want a long fuse for enough dynamite to change that!

This also brings up something to consider: as you build your team of workers and leaders, try to identify people who can "carry the ball" in introducing changes that come up. If you, the quarterback, carry the ball every time, you're going to be tackled pretty often, which is painful and frustrating. Like Jethro advised Moses (Exodus 18:17-23), you need a great deal of help! You remember my story about the five year ministry plan and the Dream Team I told about in a previous chapter? I hope you noticed that the members of the team presented the plan to the church—they presented it much more effectively than I could have, though it had my fingerprints all over it. This requires that you be willing to let other people get credit for what very well may have largely been your ideas that you planted in their willing hearts. Give yourself some time, and with changes you want to make down the road, do some seed planting and see if anything takes root. That will usually be a good indicator. Then get your team involved.

Mind Your Own Business

You cannot fix everything, and that is not your job, no matter who puts a guilt trip on you to try to get you to fill that role. Though you are certainly there to help and to lead, I would caution you to be on guard against allowing yourself to be pulled into the middle of situations that do not concern you. The best way to help a drowning person is not by going in after that person but by throwing a lifeline to them. Double drownings often happen when one person jumps in to save another, because the one who was already in trouble pulls the would-be rescuer under. Try to help as much as you can from the *outside* without trying to "jump in and fix" it. When I was younger I knew so much more than I do now! (A lot of it was incorrect, however.)

Looking back, most of the situations I tried to fix only served to get me "in a fix"! If there is a conflict or disagreement going on between a couple of other people or between a couple of groups, *do your utmost* to avoid being pulled into the midst of it, or you will most likely not come forth unscathed. A young pastor whom I knew several years ago had his first (and only) pastorate cut short because he inserted himself into the middle of a conflict which was going on in his church when he arrived. It seems that there was a room in the education building of the church which one group of ladies had been using as a craft room. Another group wanted control of that room in order to use it for another purpose. "Rev. Fix-it" went to the hardware store and purchased a new lock and installed it on the door, pocketing the key, and promptly alienated both groups and ultimately the whole church. He lost his position as pastor and is now completely out of the ministry primarily because he unthinkingly stuck his hand into that "hornets' nest." If he had considered his options, he could have referred the matter to the Building and Grounds Committee or to the deacons, or he could have tried to get the two groups to work out some kind of compromise. He could also have given the situation some time to see if it would work itself out. Taking over that problem cost him dearly.

I remember a few years ago, when there was a difficult situation going on in the church where I was pastor, a wise pastor friend said to me, "What's the worst that would happen if you just didn't do anything?" The wisdom of his question became immediately apparent to me—often, given time a situation will work out without the pastor having to "fix it." Also if you are patient, if there does turn out to be some action you need to take it will later become apparent, and you will have had time to plan your moves. Of course, if the building is on fire, you'll need to act quickly and decisively to evacuate the people, but most situations that come up do not require an immediate or authoritative response from you, if you need to act at all. At best, there are enough unseen dangers that you cannot avoid that you should *never* insert yourself or allow yourself to be pulled into a problem that does not concern you. Does that mean you close your eyes to sin? Not at all! But you can't win when you get into a position where you must pick a side or *where it looks like* you have. You must also, as in the story I told above, avoid creating *a third side*—your own—and alienating both groups. Jesus instructed the twelve before He sent them out to do ministry, "Be wise as serpents and harmless as doves" (Matthew 10:16). We still need that advice.

If you are a pastor for very long, you will one day have a couple of people in your congregation who are engaged in a conflict, and perhaps one or the other of them will ask you to help settle it, or perhaps a third party will try to get you to intervene and settle it. Jesus also gave some practical instructions about settling conflicts in the church (Matt. 18:15-18). However, be sure to keep in mind that when someone asks you to help settle a conflict, that person may really be expecting you to take his or her side, like the man who tried to get Jesus to settle a conflict with his brother over their inheritance (Lk. 12:13-14). Make it clear from the outset that the most you can do is to try and help them hear each other. On the other hand, perhaps you haven't been asked but just feel a conviction that you should approach them and try to help them get it settled. There is nothing at all wrong with your trying to help *them* settle their problem; to the contrary, that is a great thing to do *if they really want to settle it*. Just remember that *you* cannot fix it, nor can you make *them* fix it—it is up to *them*. Also they *both* must want to solve their problem or it cannot be fixed, and this almost always means that they both must be willing to give some ground. Looking back over the years, I don't remember a single situation when I went to a couple of people and tried to get them to settle a conflict, and it really worked. I also don't remember a single instance where a third person "sent" me to try to get a couple of people to reconcile, and it worked. (I don't allow myself to be "sent" anymore!) Only when both parties *themselves* have the desire can it be fixed. In the past, I have sat people down in my office and tried to make them "talk it out" and seen them go through all the motions and agree to "let bygones be bygones" with tears, handshakes, and hugs, but I've never seen it really last when it was *my* idea. *Both of them* have to really want to solve it, or it will not work. Often one person is willing, and the other is not. That doesn't work either. Jesus truly said, "Blessed are the peacemakers, for they shall be called the children of God" (Matthew 5:9). Be available and do your best to help others solve their problems, but don't take ownership of what is not yours to fix. Be careful!

Don't Play Favorites

In your flock there will be some people with whom you will immediately connect at a deep level. Perhaps you have some interest or set of views in common, or perhaps your personalities just mesh well. That is a great thing, and every pastor needs such people. However, there will be other members of your congregation with whom your connection will not come nearly so easily and effortlessly. Still others, for whatever reason, you may find challenging to make any kind of connection with at all. This does not mean that you cannot or should not form deeper relationships with some of your people than with others—it is both unavoidable and desirable that you develop a close trusting relationship with an inner circle of members of your church. These will form the nucleus of your ministry team moving forward. Remember, among the twelve, Jesus also had an inner circle—Peter, James, and John—who were allowed to share in some of Jesus' experiences, such as the raising of Jairus' daughter and the transfiguration, while the others were not. As you mentally select your team, or core group, and develop trusting relationships on a deep level with those the Lord provides to work closely with you in leading your flock down the road, you will naturally need to spend extra time with these trusted people. You must be willing invest yourself into those with whom you will be closely working down the road—but you need to be careful.

While you will not have an equal connection with and equal trust in every member of your flock, you must make sure that you show equal compassion, concern, love and acceptance to everyone without exception. You must show yourself to be equally available to each member of your flock when they have a need. Surely you will find some who are much harder to be around than others, and some with which you do not have much in common, but it may well be that these are the very people who need you the most of all. No member of your church should feel left out or ignored by the shepherd. Again, each member has unique needs as well as unique expectations, and you can never fully be everything to everyone all the time. It will take time to assess what each member expects, and the larger the flock the longer it will take to get a handle on how to treat each one. Sister Jones may not need or desire much direct attention from you, while Brother Smith wants you to check on the status of his hangnail almost daily. Again, you have to budget your time and energy, and you also must learn to distinguish between wants and needs. The starting point, however, is with what people *think they need*, and you go from there. Just be careful to make sure that no one feels neglected or that you do not care for them. Those who feel this way will never let you lead them.

Be Careful Whom You Trust

When I was in seminary we were told over and over that the ideal pastorate should last for many, many years. While a long pastorate does carry with it the opportunity to influence a particular congregation over a long period of time, hopefully enabling you to lead them a long way, there are also distinct advantages to having moved a few times. One of them is that you learn after a time or two some of the things—and people—to watch out for when you make a ministry move. When you move to another pastorate, those "problem people" from your previous church will be right there waiting for you—similar people with different faces and names, and often the issues may similar, though they can also be different. One of the great advantages you will have in a new place is that you can apply what you learned last time to a new situation, with people who may be quite similar to some you've dealt with before, but they don't know you. Your experience from the last pastorate has given you a few more "tools" to use this time. (It's good to have other options besides a hammer!) Maybe there was a difficult person last time that you could never bring on board to follow your leadership, though you tried several things that just did not work. In your new church, you have a fresh opportunity to do things differently. Over time, I have come to realize that Jesus' twelve disciples have counterparts today who are walking around in our churches! There are some Thomases, who think literally and follow the world's concept that "seeing is believing." There are a few Philips, who focus on "why we can't feed the multitude," and here and there are a few wonderful Andrews, who bring their brothers to Jesus but avoid the limelight, taking inventory and finding out what is available for Jesus to use when faced with a human need. There are also some Simon Peters, who have wonderful insight and abilities, but who may crumble when needed most, though their hearts are in the right place. There is also a Judas here and there, so be very careful whom you trust. John 2:24-25 makes it clear that Jesus was careful with regard to whom He entrusted himself. We should likewise be careful.

In the section above I mentioned that you'll need to invest yourself into those who will become your team or inner circle, with whom you will work closely, and I cautioned you to be careful. There is a second reason for this. There is an old saying among pastors, "Those who move you into the parsonage may be the ones who move you out!" Like most old sayings, it does not necessarily ring true every time, but many times it does. During your first couple of years in a pastorate, as you are "laying the foundation" and beginning to identify those who will become your inner circle or team of trusted individuals who will be instrumental in the formulation and implementation of your vision which will guide your ministry together in the coming years, you must be *extremely cautious!* There will likely be people in your congregation who help you unpack, invite you to their homes, take you to lunch, and treat you like royalty, who may have a hidden agenda. There may be others who treat you the same way, who are just genuine, kind and loving people who want to get to know their new pastor. The potential problem people can be difficult, if not impossible to detect sometimes, but if you keep your eyes and ears open, you can often spot them in the course of time, especially after you've been "around the block" a few times in the ministry. This is another reason to intentionally take a couple of years to "lay a foundation" with your people at first. If a "power broker" in the church, or a would-be power player tries to "cozy up" with you, be nice, but be cautious. People who have power usually want to keep it, and people who want power usually should not get it—especially if they want to use you to secure it. I cannot count the times that some of the people who wanted to be my "buddies" early on were people who turned out to be trouble down the road when I didn't let them control me. Often, as you learn the story of your congregation, you will find out that these very people were in the midst of the church's problems in the past, and you can take warning from what you've learned. Down the road you may find that those in your inner circle are quite different than the people you thought would be on board with you to start with. Remember something else: Jesus chose the twelve—He didn't ask for volunteers. Be careful of those who "offer."

Don't Settle for Lousy Leaders

Another closely related issue is continually keeping the wrong people in positions of leadership over the long term. In every single congregation I have served, there were people in leadership when I arrived who should never have been allowed to hold their positions in the first place. In established churches, people often tend to stake out areas of the church's programs and ministries as their "turf." As a result, in most churches there are people in leadership, not because they are doing such a wonderful job and the Lord is using them in a great way; rather, they hold their positions because sometime in the past there was a vacancy, and they filled it—ever since. Also, many times the attitude in churches is, "We just need to get *someone, whoever we can get* to take that position." It may sound cynical, but for many people, church is something they do a couple of hours a week at most, and they are just glad *they* didn't have to take the position in question. In truth, it is much better to have a vacancy in a position for a while than to have the wrong person in it. For example, if you have a person who is not doing the job they agreed to take, then another person who could really do it will not have the opportunity because the position is filled. ("Occupied" is probably a better word!) Having the wrong people in leadership is like a log-jam which hinders the flow of a river, slowing it to a trickle and turning it into a stagnant backwater. One of the most important requirements for a healthy church is to have the right people in the right positions of leadership. Often, people are allowed to be leaders because they are popular, because they belong to a prominent family, or because they have money or are successful in business, so it is erroneously assumed they will be good church leaders. Educate your people about the necessity of having faithful, reliable, and spiritually minded people who are team players in leadership. Stay alert for indicators that people are either politicking for, or are being nominated for, leadership positions for the wrong reasons. One kind of thing to listen for would be assertions like, "Our family has always been represented on the diaconate," or "I should have such and such position." Of course, the implication is that this person is entitled to leadership and power. Unfortunately, most people and many pastors don't want to "rock the boat," so they take the path of least resistance and allow these people to have their way. Then they hinder the church by occupying positions in which they either do nothing or cause trouble by pursuing their own agendas.

I vividly remember the Monday morning following deacon selection Sunday in a church I served years ago. A candidate who had not been elected showed up at my office, declaring that he and his wife were "leaving the church" because someone else had been voted in rather than him. He prevailed upon me to go home with him to console his wife, who was on the phone giving another lady in the church "an earful" about how her husband should've been selected and they were "leaving the church." After she hung up, I heard it all over again—which bought me some time to consider what my response should be. After she finished, I didn't say very much except that they were precious members of the church and, "Maybe next time the church will vote him in." I was actually *thankful* the church had not selected this man, for he proved to me by his attitude (his wife, too) that he was *not* deacon material. Sometimes, people do not realize what they are telling you by their attitudes, actions, or words. Eventually those with a personal agenda will usually give themselves away. (That couple didn't leave, either, by the way.) It goes for leadership at all levels that humility, not a sense of entitlement is a quality that should be required.

Getting the right people into leadership and keeping the wrong people out is so important that every shepherd needs to be willing to go to great lengths to accomplish this. This will likely be a process which will take several years to accomplish. Turning a church is not like turning a helicopter but is more like turning a jumbo jet, which can take miles! There are several things, none of which are quick fixes, which can be done. First, take an active role in the leadership selection process, so you can have input. Two committees a pastor should work closely with beyond the deacons or elders are the Nominating Committee (or "Enlistment Committee") and the Budget and Finance Committee. Both fill key roles in the future direction of the church. The Nominating Committee selects and enlists the volunteers who serve in almost all the leadership and committee positions in the church for the coming year. You need to be involved with this committee in order to have influence over the selection of those who will lead. Those who are selected are people *you* will have to work with for the next church year, and they need to be the right people, as much as possible. If you get involved in the committee process *before* particular names are brought up to fill positions, you can help them clarify the qualifications needed for the various positions to be filled. You can emphasize that the committee needs to select leaders who are reliable, teachable, faithful in their church involvement—people who are also growing in their walk with the Lord and gifted to suit the task. Of course this will not immediately ensure that you will now have all the right people in the right places, but it is a step in that direction. In most churches, as pastor you will not have "veto power" over any person the nominating committee chooses to select, and as an *ex officio* member of the committee you will not have a vote. However you can use your influence in the process to select appropriate people for the positions. There will always be people that the committee will want to enlist, "because they did it last year." However, if a person already has the job, and is doing nothing with it, they really shouldn't be rewarded by being allowed to just keep the title and hold things up another year. Sometimes people are put forward for leadership positions in order "to get them to come to church more." This too is a mistake and reveals the immaturity of the people who put these suggestions forward. I have *never* known anything like this to work in the long run. Actually, when I have seen marginally committed church members put into leadership positions, their level of overall church involvement is more likely to go *down* rather than up. Sometimes they assume that they have now "arrived" spiritually, so they think their low level of church involvement is fine. In other instances, I've known people who became overwhelmed by leadership responsibilities that they were not ready to handle, and I've seen such people drop away from church involvement altogether. Church members are like watermelons in one sense: if you pick them green they will not ripen. If there is any question about a person's spiritual maturity or faithfulness in church involvement, it is better to give that person some time to develop a deeper commitment before offering leadership responsibilities to him or her.   This kind of thing probably occurs in every church, and certainly we do not want to hurt people's feelings. However, we must keep the welfare of the whole church and its mission in mind. As your influence in the church grows over the years, and as you consistently stay involved in the enlistment process you can slowly get more and more of the right people in the right positions. You will always have some areas that may not have exactly the right leadership, and as the under-shepherd you will need to pay special attention to these situations and try to work with those who have the positions of leadership to help them grow and be fruitful. This gives the Lord room to work things out, which He often does in unexpected ways.

A more direct approach to help get the right kind of leaders is if you can lead the church to implement term limits, or a rotational system, on the volunteer positions in your church. In one of my pastorates, I was able to get this kind of system in place, and it worked well, particularly since we had many newer members, some of whom were mature believers with past leadership experience and gifts which they needed to use. Many churches have a three-year eligibility to serve on some or all of the committees. If you can get this expanded to include *all* the volunteer positions, you can eventually get the right people in. If there is a three-year eligibility, for example, for serving as Sunday School Director, the same person can hold the position no more than three years at a stretch, and then a new person will have a turn at the job. This also protects the church in the event that the next person is not a good fit for the position either, at worst they will only have the job for three years at the most. Another plus is that for each position, there will eventually be more than one person who knows how to do it. I remember a congregation where the church Treasurer, who had held the position for many years, died. No one else knew how to do the job, and it was a struggle to get the church's books figured out. Again, with money handling there should always be multiple people seeing and handling it for everyone's protection. It can be difficult to get a congregation to adopt a rotational policy, such as just described, so it will take a great deal of ground work and seed planting among your team and the congregation at large. It also helps if your church already has some new members who are looking for ways to become involved in the church. If people who have been deeply involved in their previous churches join your church and then find that all the leadership opportunities are closed to them, they will soon move on again to another church where they can be involved and their gifts can be used. Implementing such a plan will no doubt bring many stresses and strains, with many details to work out, and you can count on some opposition from those who've occupied comfortable positions of power for years. However, if you have the wrong people continually in leadership, the church will never be healthy. A healthy body grows, and an unhealthy body does not.

There will certainly be other potentially dangerous areas you will encounter as you shepherd our Lord's flock.   Hopefully, you will navigate your way through most of these without incident. There may be others that leave you battered and scarred, but if your focus is continually on Him, you can count on His provision and blessing as you prayerfully seek the best path on which to lead His people. My heart goes out to those who shepherd God's flock today, especially those just starting out.   I believe the ministry is harder than it was years ago when I began.   Certainly the moral parameters in our culture today are not nearly as well defined. Jesus' words to his disciples which he repeated more than

once are still relevant and helpful today: "Watch
and pray!"

Chapter 10

Planting for a Bumper Crop:
Your Preaching and Teaching Ministry

I am convinced that the single most important thing one can do as a pastor each week is to proclaim and expound the Holy Scriptures, both when the congregation gathers for worship and when they come together for study. This is also perhaps the greatest single opportunity to gain and exert influence and communicate your vision to your flock as a whole. Obviously, each of us is gifted somewhat differently, but the preaching and teaching of Biblical truth is so important that I would consider it suspect if I heard of anyone saying God had called them to pastor but not to preach and teach. In fact, I Timothy 3: 1-7, which gives qualifications for a bishop (literally "overseer", used along with "pastor" and "elder" to describe the office we hold), states that a bishop or overseer should be "apt to teach." We who are pastors are called to lead our flocks into a deepening, fulfilling relationship with the Chief Shepherd primarily by imparting spiritual truth to them, helping them to grasp its implications for their lives, and leading them to then live it out as individuals, as families, and as a congregation. This is indeed a challenge, but God has given us a wonderful, supernatural guidebook—the Holy Bible—which is an absolutely *inexhaustible* source of knowledge, guidance, and inspiration to equip believers to live out the Christian faith in a hostile world. The thrust of this chapter is not intended to provide a homiletics or teaching manual but to give a few practical pointers in how to perhaps increase the long-term effectiveness of one's pulpit and teaching ministry. In my mind, there is really no hard and fast distinction between preaching and teaching, although teaching, at least in my thinking, allows for more direct back-and-forth interaction than preaching. However, as I remember having drilled into me in homiletics classes years ago, good preaching is a dialogue, not a monologue. Suffice it to say, there is considerable overlap—good preaching teaches, and good teaching also preaches.

Let's say you're just getting started in a pastorate, either your first or maybe you've served several other churches in the past. With regard to preaching and teaching, where is the best point on the shore from which to "launch out into the deep and let down your nets for a draught?" I certainly cannot dictate to anyone what God's will for them is (I have enough trouble getting things right in my own life!), but I would recommend that early on, perhaps for the first several months I would make sure, particularly on Sunday mornings, that I give them basic, Biblical, Gospel centered messages, focusing on the central tenets of our faith. During the "getting to know you" or "laying the foundation" phase of your pastorate, as you are learning about them, they are also becoming acquainted with you. The most important thing they can ever learn about you is what you believe about sin, salvation, and Jesus Christ. I don't think I've ever actually announced this as a Sunday morning sermon series, but I can see great benefit to a carefully arranged sequence of messages around the theme: "What is the Gospel?" Doubtless most of them are already Christians and know the basics from having been in the church for years; however, they will surely be keenly interested to know, what the Gospel is, *according to you!* It cannot be overemphasized that gaining their trust on this point will become the cornerstone of the foundation of trust you hope to build with them and from which you will lead the flock in the future. If they trust you here, it will *greatly help them trust you in the other areas of your ministry with them!* It is also a great strategy, whether you announce it or not as a sermon series, particularly while you are new, to address that which *every person on earth* needs. At this time particularly, if you "hit a home run" the bases are sure to be loaded, and the long-term effect of these early messages can stretch far beyond the Sundays during which they are preached. Again, unless you know their previous pastor you really do not know exactly *what* they've been hearing. Moreover, there may have been some difficult times for the church toward the end of the previous pastor's tenure or during the interim period when the flock had no full-time shepherd. The greatest healing balm and the most wonderful source of unity at our disposal is the wonderful saving grace of God in Jesus Christ. It is also true that although you may have been told some of their story in process with the Search Committee, you really do not know what the theological issues really are in this church, especially with regard to where there may have been doctrinal controversies. I certainly would *not recommend* starting out by going into your view on the millennium! You don't know what they've already been told, and there are different views on this among equally devout believers. Start with the basics—the Gospel—through which both the members and guests will get a window on what you believe about God, sin and judgment, humanity, grace, Jesus Christ and His incarnation and atonement, human responsibility, and heaven and hell, just to mention a few things. It is a wise shepherd who emphasizes that which is central to the faith, rather than that which is peripheral. As in a lake, the "danger zones" theologically are most often in "shallow waters." The most fertile ground in your spiritual field will be the rich soil of the incarnation, atonement, and resurrection, through which the wonderful transforming grace of God is made available to us all. For me, a great percentage of the time I've spent in the pulpit has been invested into these great truths throughout each of my pastorates, particularly on Sunday mornings. I say Sunday mornings, because in most churches, at least if they're like the ones I have served, you will be addressing the most diversified group of the whole week then. You will have your faithful workers; you'll have the marginally involved who only come Sunday mornings; you'll have a few other members who only attend once in a while; and you will have some guests and hopefully first-time newcomers who may not be Christians yet. It is a good rule of thumb to stick to the basics on Sunday mornings for this very reason. That doesn't mean I don't ever take a "sermon series" approach, or preach through a book of the Bible on Sunday mornings. I just make sure that when I do it focuses on the Gospel, which everyone young and old needs. I think Spurgeon once said something like, "The same simple Gospel which saves sinners feeds saints."

Although many churches have discontinued Sunday evening worship, this remains my favorite church gathering of the whole week. Usually the crowd is smaller (sometimes *much* smaller). There was only one congregation I have served where the gathering was as large on Sunday evenings as on Sunday mornings, and it was also the church that grew the most, where we had to do so much building, as described earlier. The excitement was so great there that people didn't want to miss what might happen by not being there. Though you may have fewer people, Sunday evenings present a great preaching and especially a *teaching* opportunity. At this service, those regular in attendance will also most likely be your faithful workers and leaders who carry the major load of what goes on in the church week by week. To keep up their energy level, it is important that they be fed with the richest spiritual nutrition you can dig out of the Scriptures. On Sunday nights you can delve into the deep things of God and really help your workers grow in their faith. They *need* the "meat" rather than "milk," because as faithful workers and leaders they are truly serious about living out their faith both as individuals and in the corporate life of the flock. Also your preaching/teaching ministry can become a major motivator for your people as it becomes a valuable vehicle for imparting *your vision* to them. As you hold up for them a Biblical picture of what faithfulness and fruitfulness looks like, you are also imparting to them a glimpse at first, and eventually a panoramic view of how you envision "the Promised Land," the life of your shared ministry "flowing with milk and honey." You will also be preparing them for the rigors of the journey, which may realistically include some "wilderness" between here and there. Though I have served a couple of churches which did not gather for services on Sunday evenings, It is well worth the time and effort it will take on your part to have them, and doing so can pay great dividends in your leadership of God's flock. After all, it's fifty-two more times over the course of a year for the body to be together, feeding on the Word of God, and that provides the opportunity for a great deal of potential good for His flock.

Another opportunity available in most churches is a midweek Bible study, usually on Wednesday evenings, which you can also capitalize on as a great teaching avenue. Here again, most in attendance will be your faithful workers and leaders, though if your church has a "family night" during this time some of your workers will be involved perhaps in leading groups of children or youth. Still, it is a great time to explore a carefully chosen book of the Bible or to provide a "survey," perhaps of the four Gospels and how they relate to each other, or to work your way through the history of the Old Testament. I have been particularly encouraged over the years with the feedback I have received in response to the Old Testament books I have taught. Many people who've been Christians for years have never known the practical wisdom, the wealth of color, and the wonderful depth of God's truth to be found there. Other than the stories of Jesus and of the early church, found in the Gospels and Acts, my favorite Bible characters and stories are practically all to be found in the Old Testament. Many of the "senior saints" faithful on Sunday and Wednesday evenings, are eager to renew acquaintance with "old friends" from the pages of the Old Testament, and many younger believers can be pleasantly surprised at the up-to-date relevance of this often overlooked but valuable Record, as ancient people and their interactions with God are brought to life again before their eyes. Sadly, in our age of technology, many of our people do not know much about the Bible, since people have so many options for entertainment and do not read much. The potential fruitfulness is unlimited when you invest all this truth into people's lives, particularly when you consider its cumulative effect over the years.

Hopefully, there will also be other, though maybe not regularly scheduled, opportunities to impart God's truth, share your God-given vision, and motivate your people to move forward at various times during the year. Some of these might be, for example, a three or four-night special study of some book of the Bible, some Christian doctrine, or perhaps practical training which you can provide with regard to financial stewardship or soul-winning. There are also many kinds of discipleship materials available, perhaps through your denomination, many of which are of great value and easily adaptable for congregations of many sizes or for small groups. There are many approaches to a viable teaching and discipleship ministry. You will have to discern the path He has for you. Remember, just because I do things one way does not mean that some other approach will not work better for you. Having said this, I would urge you to emphasize your preaching and teaching ministry in the path God leads you and take advantage of whatever regular and other opportunities to get the truth of God into the lives of people. One of my bedrock convictions of which I am absolutely convinced is that if I can whet people's appetites to "stick their noses" into the Bible and study it on their own it will absolutely change their lives, as it has mine.

Every preaching and teaching opportunity is a chance to influence people to either begin following Jesus, to follow Him more closely, to share your vision of where He is leading, and to motivate your flock to be willing to move forward in anticipation of the vision they've caught from you becoming a reality. It also provides strength and resolve for the journey and prepares them for the challenges that lie ahead. The strength and quality of your leadership as a shepherd will to a great degree go hand-in-hand with the investment you make in developing and using your abilities and opportunities as preacher and teacher. Plow deeply, plant liberally, water faithfully, cultivate carefully, and you can expect one day to harvest abundantly!

Chapter 11

A Cord of Three Strands:
Building a Strong and Healthy Church

"A cord of three strands is not easily torn apart"
(Ecclesiastes 4:12b, NASB).

Every under-shepherd is unique in many ways. We each
are gifted differently, and we each have different life-
stories that have shaped us as individual ministers. We also
do not all share the same interests, the same perspectives on
many things, or the same strengths and weaknesses in many
of the various facets of our work. Some of us are more
naturally gifted as caregivers, while others are more driven
to lead their flocks forward toward the "green pastures,
with another group being most passionate about preaching
and teaching. The same kind of thing is true for each
church member and for the local congregation. Every
congregation, like every believer, including pastors, is
special and precious to our Lord, and each local body of
believers has the potential to excel in at least one particular
area of congregational ministry and likewise will have
some areas of deficiency, which need to be strengthened.
In the first of the nine "summary accounts" in the Book of
Acts (2:42-47), the New Testament provides a window into
the life of the earliest church, painting a picture which
emphasizes three "activities" (which I'll use for lack of a
better word, since I'll be focusing primarily on what *the
people* rather than God was doing) as central in the life of
the early Jerusalem church shortly after Pentecost. These
three "activities" which were part and parcel of the daily
lives of the people in this fledgling congregation are

exactly the same "activities" which in a healthy church today must be woven together, like "a cord of three strands," to provide balance and strength for the body, fostering an atmosphere in which we can depend upon our Lord to bless and to "add to the church, the ones being saved" (Acts 2:47).

The first "activity" in the Jerusalem church had to do with apostolic teaching. Verse 42 tells us that the people "continued steadfastly in the apostles' doctrine ("teaching"). This tells us that the earliest church was *both a teaching and a learning church!* Again, we can never fully divorce our "activities" as believers from what our Lord through the Holy Spirit is doing, since He is the actual teacher when real spiritual truth is imparted and received. However, my point is that if the exciting, miraculous life that is portrayed in this Scripture passage is ever going to again happen in a local congregation, we who are under-shepherds must focus on developing a strong teaching ministry in our congregations, which feeds our flocks on the deep spiritual truth recorded for us by the Apostles concerning our Lord Jesus Christ and what it means to be His disciples and His Church. The Church is not an organization but an *organism!* Just as God was incarnate in the fully divine and fully human Jesus Christ, our risen Lord is again clothed in human flesh in His wonderful, miraculous body—the Church! (I don't understand all I know about this!) We cannot create a hunger for the Word of God, but His Spirit who indwells them can, and He does with those who are truly His! The old saying "You can lead a horse to water, but you can't make him drink!" is partly true. However, if you keep bringing him to the trough, there's a good chance that he'll eventually get thirsty! It has amazed me in every single congregation I have served that the more I've focused on developing a strong teaching ministry, not only through my own teaching but also by training and equipping others in the church for teaching, the more people have grown genuinely hungry for God and His Word. While saving faith is much more than having the right information and giving mental assent to it, there is basic, foundational content to the Christian faith. In the pluralistic culture of our day, the members of our flocks desperately need to be firmly rooted in sound doctrine in order to live out their faith in a hostile world. They need to know what they believe—and *why*. In a theological education, Systematic Theology is a required course, or at least it should be. Your preaching and teaching ministry can likewise help the members of your flock see how the different facets of the Christian faith fit together in a systematic, balanced way. A Godly professor of mine years ago, used to regularly draw a pie chart on the blackboard, divided into equally sized pieces, to illustrate how what we believe, for example, about God should be balanced with what we believe about humanity. Likewise with sin and salvation, etc. the pieces, which balanced one another out, were opposite each other in the chart. Helping your people see how the components of the Christian faith fit together as a whole greatly helps prepare them to both face temptation and bear witness to Christ effectively. It can be a daunting task, especially in a church that does not have a history of *teaching* pastors, but developing a strong teaching ministry is an indispensible ingredient in developing a healthy church.

The second "activity" of the people we see going on in Acts 2:42-47 is worship. After verse 42 lists "fellowship" (which we'll talk about later, since it is really produced by the work of the Holy Spirit), we are told that they continued also in "breaking of bread, and in prayers." Many New Testament scholars understand "breaking of bread" as a reference to the Lord's Supper, which is a central practice in true worship, instituted and commanded by our Lord and recognized throughout the many Christian denominations as either an ordinance or a sacrament. In Luke/Acts as well as the Pauline writings this expression several times appears to suggest "gathering at our Lord's table" and remembering, reenacting, and reliving collectively as His Church, the awfulness of our sins and the depth of His love in His dying our death, taking our punishment, and with his "broken body and shed blood" paying for all our sins, which is proven by His victorious resurrection. "Prayers" also refer to our hearts' open conversation with God, made possible by our Savior and stimulated by His Holy Spirit. Together "breaking of bread" and "prayers" encapsulates what is the essence of worship for the Church—experiencing communion (oneness) with our Lord and lifting our very beings up to Him in reverent thanksgiving, and praise for His gracious acceptance of us! In true worship, we open ourselves to Him like a flower on the windowsill opens its petals to the morning sun. What a powerful and transforming experience as we respond to the One who gave Himself for us by freely giving ourselves to Him! A healthy church will also be a church that truly worships "in Spirit and in truth." Neither empty ritualism on the one hand or unbridled emotion on the other characterizes genuine worship, which is at the same time both reverent and exhilarating, with Christ receiving all the glory. No believer or congregation can be healthy apart from a life of true worship.

The third essential "activity" of a healthy body of believers portrayed in this first summary statement is ministry—the use of all available resources of any kind for the meeting of every kind of human needs. Here we are told that believers were so united in focus and commitment that they liquidated their material goods and distributed them to all who were in need (verses 44-45). It is worth noting here that the verb tenses in the Greek text are imperfect, indicating continual, regular action. It is true that the situation in Jerusalem was unusual: The Church was born on Pentecost, with the town being full of Jewish people, many of whom had come from far and wide, doubtless with many having made the journey for the first (and only) time in their lives. These non-Palestinean or Hellenistic Jews formed a sizeable portion of the church, and since they were far from home, they had no housing, jobs, or other means of providing the day-to-day essentials of life for themselves. The church stepped into the gap, with members who were able, sacrificially providing for the needs of both these new believers as well as for anyone else in need. What a wonderful way of demonstrating the love of God, which was being "shed abroad" in their hearts by the Holy Spirit! Imagine the doors that were opened for the Gospel to be shared as those newly converted believers cheerfully shared both their material and spiritual "wealth" with those who were in need. Every time food or clothing, or shelter was given, it opened up an opportunity to share *the reason* behind this gift—the "unspeakable gift" of God to the world—His Son Jesus Christ, through whom we can all have forgiveness and eternal life! True Christian ministry is *always* concerned with bringing the Gospel, which Paul said is "the power of God unto salvation to everyone who believes" (Romans 1:16), to bear upon all those He puts in our path to help. That doesn't mean we're supposed to "pounce" on everyone we try to help; rather, we prayerfully allow the Holy Spirit to provide an open door so we can share. In Acts 8, we are given a picture of how the Holy Spirit can do this, as He positions Philip on the desert road and arranges things so that the Ethiopian is reading aloud from Isaiah 53 (Reading prior to the modern era was almost always done orally.) when his chariot passes by, giving Philip a wonderful starting point from which to evangelize him. The way souls are won is that God the Holy Spirit places His hand upon both parties and brings them together at just the right time! Just as a lake or pond must have both an inlet source for fresh water as well as a spillway through which it can overflow, a church must not only "take in" the wonderful grace of God through teaching and worship but also overflow into the lives of others with ministry to all human needs, in the hope not only of *improving* the quality of their lives temporarily but also of sharing the Gospel which will *transform* their lives eternally. It is indeed sad that many churches do little or no planned, intentional ministry in their larger communities. Every church should operate both short term and on-going ministries to involve the members. Remember how Jesus involved the disciples in distributing the loaves and fishes? What a learning moment for them when 12 baskets of fragments were gathered afterward—one for each disciple! Our people will find fulfillment in being involved in ministry to human needs that cannot be found anywhere else. In a large portion of congregations, members are sent forth after worship, "with a wink and a nod" to "serve the Lord," with no tangible plans and no real expectation that much will be done in the way of ministry or witness during the week. No wonder so many churches are struggling! For many believers, being "mission minded" means that they donate money here and there to "missions," never considering that we are all commissioned to be our Lord's emissaries to a suffering and lost world that begins at the church door! While I'm at it, many churches in effect label large sums of money "corban" (Mark 7:11) by hoarding it in "designated funds" which they have no real plans to use, making such money unavailable to use for meeting human needs. Churches that do this usually have substituted a "business model" for the Biblical model given in Scripture, by which we are to operate. A business operates on the principle of profit and loss, with the goal of taking in more capital than is spent, accumulating a profit. The church is supposed to operate by faith, which means we are to use *everything* we have (which is really His anyway) in ministry, trusting him to provide our needs in the process (remember the 12 baskets of fragments?). We are His body—the *only* body He has to feed the hungry, help the sick, or reach out to the downtrodden—or reach the lost! In just about every church I have served, when I first began talking about "outreach ministry," they seemed to think I was talking about going door-to-door and inviting people to church! True outreach ministry is what we as a church do to help meet people's immediate needs in the community around us, *whatever those needs are,* in order to both help them in a temporal way as well as to win a hearing for the Gospel, as they wonder why we are so generous to them. Every healthy church will continually conduct both on-going ministries as well as short-term projects aimed at special needs and crisis situations that come up in their community. It is through these expressions of compassion and love that doors are opened for the Gospel. As a pond becomes stagnant without a working spillway, so a church becomes stagnant if it does not continuously overflow in ministry to the surrounding community. No church can be healthy without continual, intentional ministry to human needs in the larger community.

You will have noticed in looking at the Scripture passage we have been drawing from that there is much more happening than the three "activities" I have discussed. Practically everything else going on was produced by the work of the Holy Spirit as the apostolic teaching, worship, and ministry went on. The first thing to be mentioned is "fellowship" back in verse 42. The root meaning of the Greek word from which this is translated means "common." True Christian fellowship is much more than eating fried chicken together in a "fellowship hall!" It is the *commonality* we as believers have together through the Holy Spirit, who at the same time indwells each one of us and flows through us corporately as Christ's body, the Church, reproducing the life of Jesus in both our individuality and our togetherness all over again, so we can show Him to the world in a unified, consistent way. We also see in verse 43 that there was "fear" (reverence), and that "signs and wonders" ("Exodus" language!) were done through the apostles. In a church where we fully devote ourselves, or "continue steadfastly" in the three "activities" described above, miraculous things will indeed happen which no one can explain, and an atmosphere of reverence will permeate our congregations, as we are in awe of what God is doing. We are also told about their unity, about being together daily, "with one accord", and "breaking bread from house to house with gladness and singleness of heart." If we can lead our congregations to focus on teaching and learning, worship, and ministry, it gives the Holy Spirit a great deal of room to produce all kinds of blessings among His people, more than we can imagine!. Perhaps most wonderful of all is the real prospect of souls saved and lives being changed day by day!   I've experienced a taste of this, and I can now never be satisfied with anything less!

As a final thought, when a congregation continually gives itself to Apostolic teaching, worship, and ministry, each "strand' in that rope strengthens the other two! Consider how an atmosphere of teaching and learning is enhanced, when believers' hunger for the truth is stimulated by their intention to *share* the insights they are gaining as well as the realization that the church's teaching ministry is not just so they will have more information but to give them *preparation* to go out together and serve the Lord in practical ways that are already prepared. Likewise, the teaching and ministry going on in the church informs and strengthens worship. As people learn more of the deep truths of Scripture, this enables them to worship at deeper levels as they grasp more and more of the majesty of the One with Whom we have to do. The fervency of our prayers, praise, and the glorifying of our wonderful God becomes almost *electric* when we're getting ready to go out and serve Him again together in tangible, coordinated, intentional ways this week, especially having gotten a taste of how He can use us from last week! It also multiplies our anticipation in worship, when there are new people there to whom we demonstrated God's love in tangible ways and with whom we shared the Gospel during the previous week, who have now come to make their faith public and unite with the body! Finally, ministry is fueled by both the teaching and worship experiences we share together. This is what sets the church apart from a "service organization." The teaching/learning and worship focus our hearts on Christ and the Gospel and fill our hearts to share *Him* through every act of kindness and mercy as well as verbally sharing the Good News. A church that is truly given to these three things will not have much to fuss about—they will be captivated by all the wonderful things that the Lord is doing in and through His people. This is indeed a cord of three strands that is not easily torn apart.

Chapter 12

On the Desert Road:
Developing a Support System

In the previous chapter I briefly referred to the story of Philip and the Ethiopian recorded in Acts 8. Philip had been preaching Christ in Samaria and receiving a wonderful response to his message when he was divinely instructed to leave this exciting situation, walk about fifty miles to the south beyond Jerusalem, and get on "the desert road," which would've been a dry, lonely, desolate place, especially in comparison to the excitement that was going on in Samaria. Often in ministry, times of excitement and obvious fruitfulness and blessing will give way to "desert road" periods when we find ourselves exhausted and alone, wondering why. Let's not forget that Philip was not told any more of God's plan until the chariot carrying the Ethiopian came rumbling by! There is much we cannot know in advance about God's plan for us, and during those lonely times it is wonderful to be assured that He is still with us and has our situation well in hand. Shepherding our Lord's flock can be a lonely task, even though we're often surrounded with people in our congregations. Part of the problem is that they will not understand, nor can they, since being "one of the sheep" is quite different than being a shepherd. In a pastor's work, there are many things for you to carry that can become quite heavy, involving the members of your flock, as well as congregational situations and issues that are ongoing. On the one hand, there are sicknesses, marital situations, other family issues, and such things as moral lapses that command a great deal of your attention and compassion and can be quite draining upon your energy level. Couple these things with week-to-week congregational situations, such as conflicts, power issues, or difficulties resulting from leaders who drop the ball, and you can almost be overwhelmed at times. These are just some of the regular "maintenance" issues that come up in the ministry. When you add the stress of gathering a "team" or "core group" of trusted members in whom you're trying to get your vision to take root and through whom you hope to introduce major changes into the life of the congregation, the load can increase exponentially, especially since no one in your church can really appreciate all that you have on you. Then when you factor in the opposition, much of which will be covert and not out in the open, if you're not careful, you can be crushed by the cumulative weight of things that no else realizes.

During those lonely "desert road" times, our Lord always makes available sources of refreshment, and we must keep our eyes open for those often "hidden springs" as well as unexpected "chariots of opportunity" that pass by. I don't really know how to explain it, but often in the midst of these difficult times an unexpected ministry opportunity comes along which brings with it the realization, "Look! Here is water" (Acts 8:26)! How refreshing after a fifty mile hike *through the desert,* to have the opportunity get into the water and baptize that guy—and be refreshed in the process! If we also take a look at the Old Testament, it is highly instructive that during the darkest period of Elijah's ministry, when Jezebel had, as it were, a "wanted dead or alive" poster out on him, that in the midst of his discouragement God reminded him that he was not really alone, but there were seven thousand others in Israel who remained faithful. He was then sent to find a helper who would partner with him in ministry and carry the work on when he was gone (I Kings 19:16-21). My point here is that everyone who shepherds God's people needs support from others who help us remember that we are not alone, and some can really share the load with us and maybe even continue the work we've begun after we are gone. There are also other ways to lighten the load temporarily, which can give us needed respite along the way, and here are a few ideas that may help.

The first and most important component of a dependable support system is our Lord Himself. He always knows what you're experiencing and how you feel, and He always cares. What is more, He's always with you, and He always has a plan for getting you through. It is highly instructive that in both stories referred to above, both Philip and Elijah were attuned to hear God speak and direct them when His Word came. It is always important for us to be in close fellowship with Christ, but it is crucial during the difficult and lonely periods of ministry, when we struggle with feelings of discouragement. Both of these men were given new and important ministry opportunities, which no doubt helped them have a renewed perspective—and renewed strength. It is not by accident that the second chapter of this book was about cultivating a close walk with the Lord. I won't plow too deep here, since we've already gone over it, but in the ministry there will be times when *no one else* understands. Jesus is always there to help, and our walk with Him is the key to everything. Stay close to Him.

The second most important part of your support system is your family, also discussed at length in the fourth chapter. Again, suffice it to say that there will be times when things are going on in your church or in your life that the only ones who will understand and will stand with you are your family and particularly your spouse. I've said it all before but cultivate strong relationships within your family and especially with your mate and protect those relationships at all costs. They don't have a pastor—only you—and there will be times when you have only them. You all need each other. I still remember, though it was many years ago, how lonely it was much of the time during the five years I was a pastor before the Lord brought my wonderful wife to me! And how often the Lord has used her to lift me up, as when I've needed to be (figuratively speaking) "brought home on a stretcher" after some deacons' meeting! Surely she is "bone of my bones, and flesh of my flesh!" (Genesis 2:23). What would we do without our families—and our spouses!

It is also crucial that we develop close friendships with a few carefully chosen minister friends. Proverbs 27:17 says, "Iron sharpeneth iron; so a man sharpeneth the countenance of his friend." It is especially true in the ministry that good friends "keep us sharp!" I am so thankful that God has brought several wise and Godly Christian ministers into my life with whom meaningful friendships have developed, some for shorter periods of time, but a few with whom I've grown closer and closer over many years. They are among the most treasured blessings of God that have come to me in my whole life. Some of these were older and wiser college and seminary professors, many of whom had a great deal of "in the field" experience as pastors or missionaries which made them great role models, mentors, and confidants. Others were veteran pastors with years of shepherding experience under their belts whom the Lord placed around me in my earlier years to help guide and encourage me along the path of ministry. Many of both groups just mentioned are now part of the "great cloud of witnesses" who have finished their race and are now in the grandstand cheering the rest of us on as we "run with patience the race that is set before us, looking unto Jesus," who Himself waits to greet us at the finish line (Hebrews 12:1-2)! My main goal in writing this book is my heart's desire to pass on to others as much as I can of the wisdom and insight I have been freely given by many others who have travelled the path longer and farther than I. Heaven looks better all the time! Not only because I'll be with Jesus, but also because I'll be reunited with *all the precious people* who've meant so much in my life who are already there! Thankfully there are other, equally precious pastor friends God has blessed me with who are still here, from whose cisterns of wisdom and experience I can draw clear waters that refresh and enlighten me. Some of these are confidants with whom I communicate quite often, and we share our individual and mutual burdens together. In particular, a couple of pastor friends along with their wives and children are like family to us. We are close; our wives are close; and our children consider themselves as "cousins!" Interestingly, my two closest pastor friends are *quite* different from one another in their perspectives and views about many things. One of these close friends and I agree in most of our views, and he generally is quite helpful to me in situations where I need to be reminded that "I'm really not crazy or an idiot" or whenever I need encouragement to "stay on course" with what I know I need to do. Like a second person who can help you see where a jigsaw puzzle piece may fit, he often helps me see other steps I need to take or avoid. Also, knowing we both struggle in many of the same areas gives me (and hopefully him, too) great comfort in knowing I'm not alone. An even more interesting thing to me is that my other closest pastor friend has views and perspectives about many things that are different from mine. I have learned over the years, whenever I "get in a jam" in a ministry situation to *always find out what he thinks*. Without fail, he *always* helps me see things from a *different* vantage point, and in the process he raises issues, gives insight, and often suggests possible actions or solutions I would've never, ever considered. Many times, I've ended up following his sage advice, thanking God for the potholes this friend has helped me avoid and the successes he's helped bring about. Both of these two priceless friends were guys with whom I connected during college or seminary days. While the last thing I would do is to diminish the value of the classroom preparation I received for the ministry, with no hesitation I would have to say that the most valuable portion of all that I gained in my formal theological education was the friendships with treasured role models, mentors, and friends. They are absolutely indispensible! Be sure you cultivate these relationships and protect them carefully.

Another important component of a healthy support system or "safety net" in ministry is the friendships that one can develop within the congregations you serve. It is true that as a shepherd there are always things you carry around with you that no one in your congregation should know about, often for reasons of confidentiality. Often, even if they did know they wouldn't be able to fully understand. However, this does not mean that you shouldn't develop close friendships within the flock. To the contrary, as you build your team or "core group" of trusted ministry partners with and through whom you hope to formulate a ministry vision and get it to take root in your congregation, you will be developing close friendships with these trusted laypeople. In every church I've served, I've made it a point to try to have at least a couple of friends whom I can really trust. With these trusted members of the flock, whenever I'm considering trying to introduce something new I will "run it by" them first, before I "launch out into the deep" with it. This way I can get feedback ahead of time, so I'll know whether I need to fine-tune what I want to do or maybe discard it altogether. (You always want to "get the bugs out" before you present *anything* to the church for approval!) One of the keys to almost everything in the ministry is to *take a team approach.* On the one hand, it distributes the weight of the work *and* the potential blessings among more people as others are involved in the process. At the same time, it provides a needed protection against one of the most common causes of ministerial "paralysis" which a pastor can face: *isolation.* One of the greatest benefits of partnering with others in shared ministry relationships is that once you're gone on to another field of service, these particular friendships will often grow even deeper and stronger over the succeeding years, once the pastor/parishioner dynamic is taken out of the equation. Over the years, among my most valued friends on earth are people with whom friendships blossomed as we "took faith risks" together, serving our Lord as pastor and church members. We are bound together, not only by our common experiences and mutual memories but by the sustained realization of the value we continue to have for each other in our present lives. In each congregation we have served, Jennifer and I have a few cherished friends with whom we are still quite close; although we've made sure upon leaving a congregation that we've given plenty of time and space for the next pastor to get established relationally. Usually these friends, once we've left, are people we probably won't see for a year or two, since we're no longer close by and we're all busy as we travel our separate paths. Those with whom we're still close today are those with whom we've renewed our fellowship through various circumstances over the years, because we've come to realize that we still need and value each other. I have found that proven friends who are valuable in my present pastorate as we serve side-by-side have often become some of my most important life-long friends after the Lord has moved us on. Some of these are even more valuable sources of insight today than I found them before, especially when I need an objective layman's perspective, which is always relevant for me to know. As we've said before, ministry takes place in the context of relationships. The development of meaningful friendships in your present pastorate and especially friendships that endure over the years with people from previous churches are among the most reliable evidences that your ministry has borne lasting fruit.

Finally, there are a few other valuable sources of refreshment that should not be neglected if a pastor is going to "stay sharp" and be most effective. Every pastor needs to try to take a day off each and every week *if at all possible.* You cannot afford to wait for "a stopping place," for there are none in the ministry. There will always be needs to address, preparations to make, and a multitude of other tasks begging for your attention. It is crucial that you carve out regular blocks of time to temporarily lay aside your burdens. Every pastor needs to regularly do *something* that does not have a bearing on some else's eternal soul. Many pastors find diversion in "chasing a golf-ball around the course," or fishing, or woodworking, or something else. In the ministry, there are many things that you cannot really measure—you're trying to build the lives of people, which involves the investment of many intangible things on your part. If you rely upon statistical information, such as how many baptisms you administered last year, you may become quite discouraged when you consider how many of these people who were added to your church did not seem to last. At least you can keep up with your golf score—which might be discouraging, too! It really does help for a pastor to regularly do something for which the results are visible and obvious. How you arrange to do it is between you and Him, but for me Fridays, during which I usually fly-fish, have worked pretty well over the years. By that time in the week, both my sermons for Sunday have already had all the ingredients "added and mixed" (at least usually). Like a cake, a sermon needs to be "put in the oven" awhile before it is served, and Friday and Saturday generally provide enough time for what I have prepared earlier in the week to be "done." Meanwhile as I'm focusing on other things, the nutrition, flavor, and temperature of my weekly messages can reach their peak. In addition to a day off, let me urge you be sure to use all your vacation each year. I failed at this for most of my years in the ministry. I grew up on a chicken farm, so I didn't grow up in a family that took vacations. (Chickens like to be fed every day!) I never took a vacation in my first pastorate until the fifth year—I say this not to boast but to warn. We cannot stay fresh without some extended time off now and then. Likewise our people often need a break too! It will do them good, and it can be *crucial for you and your family* to take adequate time off. I have gone through several periods of near burnout in the ministry, which in retrospect might have been avoided if I had taken adequate vacation time through the years. Take care of yourself and your family, and you can take much better care of your flock.

Chapter 13

Landing the Plane: Concluding a Pastorate

When you take a trip on an airliner, the most important factor determining the quality of your flight is the landing. No matter how beautiful the scenery below you, how breathtaking the sky and clouds above and around you, or how smooth the ride, if you crash and burn your flight will not have been a good one! The same thing is true of a pastorate. No matter how wonderful your sermons have been, how many hospital visits you have made, or even how many people came into the church during your tenure, if you "crash and burn" your ministry with that congregation will largely not be well remembered, either. Finishing well is of primary importance when any project is undertaken. Consider the old saying which I believe goes back to Franklin, about the "want of a nail" resulting in the successive losses of a shoe, a horse, a rider, a battle, and finally a war! I wonder if the "want of a nail" came about because the smith did not quite finish his job? Jesus did His best to instill in the twelve—and in all believers—the importance of faithfulness to the end of our lives—of finishing well (Mark 13:13). He also stressed this in His own life and, especially at the crucifixion, with His last words: "It is finished" (John 19:30). The great Apostle Paul also gives us a similar example reflected in these words, shortly before the end of his life: "I have fought a good fight, I have finished my course, I have kept the faith" (II Timothy 4:7). While it is vitally important that we finish our lives well by being faithful to the end, it is also crucial that each segment of our life's work be brought to a graceful and positive conclusion as well. I have known several otherwise fine pastors who in one way or another "snatched defeat from the jaws of victory" by ending a pastorate with wreckage, as it were, scattered all over the airfield, and bruised and battered people being carried off on litters because they failed to finish well. Without a doubt, shepherding a flock is exceedingly difficult work, and the frustrations are many. It is also an alarming fact that many pastors today find themselves in situations where they are subject to being so marginalized by the powers that be that they either leave their churches out of pure misery or else they are forcibly removed if they do not choose to leave on their own. That being true, it is incumbent upon us to be cognizant of both *when* to leave and *how* to leave.

Knowing When to Leave

First, let me begin with a word of warning: A ministry move is *not* the same thing as a career move. Go back and read that again! Just because First Baptist Church—a much larger, more prestigious congregation which pays double your salary—has contacted you about the possibility of your coming and being *their* pastor—that does not constitute *the call of God* for you to do that. There *was* a time—when I was much younger and our daughter was small—that churches sometimes contacted me to see if I was interested in coming and being their pastor. I practically always "put the fleece out" and checked into it to see what kind of opportunity it was, but Jennifer and I never pursued any of these "opportunities" unless we *already knew* we were in the process of finishing our work in our present congregation. You might also be interested to know, only two of our ministry moves involved going to a larger church than the one we were currently serving.

The other occasions involved going to churches that were either comparable in size or smaller than the congregations we currently served. It has been many years since a church sought after me, since I am no longer of a "marketable" age. This points up the sad fact (mentioned earlier in another context) that many churches follow a business model rather than a Biblical model of operation. Not only do they operate on the principle of profit and loss, when seeking a pastor they take essentially the approach that a business corporation takes in hiring a manager. Often, congregations seek after a younger pastor, thinking they can fit him into their mold, or perhaps they think this will "get young people back into our church." Another symptom of this problem is that such churches essentially see their members as recipients of ministry rather than as agents of ministry to the larger community. They tend to view the pastor as an employee who is there to do their bidding, rather than as an emissary of God who's been sent lead them to engage the community in ministry and witness. It is a sad commentary on the spiritual climate among churches today that once you're beyond fifty years of age, fewer and fewer churches will seriously consider you as a viable candidate for their next pastor, though you have more skill, experience, and wisdom than ever. It often comes about that a church with serious internal problems and conflicts ends up with a novice pastor who unknowingly complicates the situation, not having the expertise required to avoid ending up on one side of a controversy or the other—or (as mentioned earlier) creating *a third faction.* Even so, the Lord graciously loves congregations which are "off the tracks" in these and other ways, and He blesses them in every way that He can. Graciously He often does arrange for Godly, conscientious, wise under-shepherds to become the pastors of unhealthy churches in order to lead them back to the right path. In truth, every congregation I have served has been infected with the worldly, business model way of thinking to some degree. Most of them over time responded at least partially to my consistent and patient attempts to lead them to truly walk by faith and not by sight. The most difficult church I have served, where I was and still am convinced God also placed me, was the most tied to a worldly, business model of operation of any church I served, and of all my pastorates I was able to effect the least change in a Kingdom direction there. As in Nazareth of old, Jesus "did not many mighty works there because of their unbelief" (Matthew 13:58). This also serves to illustrate that God will not always send you to a healthy church when He moves you, but many times He will place you in an unhealthy congregation, which is exactly where you are *needed.* In fact, knowing you're needed is one of the ways you recognize a church to which He is leading you, as we've mentioned before. A true ministry move can be either to a larger or a smaller church, with larger or smaller compensation, and to a healthy or unhealthy congregation, but it must be an act of faith on your part to go there, and you need to be sure God is calling you to serve Him there.

Another related word of warning is this: God is not bound to lead you directly from one pastorate to another. What I mean here is that it really does happen that it may be time to conclude a pastorate, and you may not have another congregation to immediately go and serve. I recognize that God's path for each of us is unique in many ways and tailored to our individual abilities and needs. I also realize that every one of us needs to make a living and we all need to have some avenue for providing for our families. Recognizing that His plan for each of us is in many ways different, my own experience has been that three of my pastorates have been concluded *without* my having in hand another church to serve. It is also part of my life experience, and I believe part of God's *preparation of me* for the ministry, that I worked as a carpenter with my father for twelve years after high school. I believe God planned for me to have a marketable skill against the day when I would be required (more than once) to conclude a pastorate and not be able to directly move on to another congregation. I also know and have previously known other pastors who have had similar experiences, not to mention others who found themselves forced out of pastorates one way or another, several having to struggle greatly to take care of their families. Remember, it will cost you to serve the Lord; though it will inevitably cost much more not to. Whatever God's plan may be for you, it is worthwhile to be forewarned that the day may well come when you have to take an unforeseen step of faith in concluding a pastorate and have to do something else until another opportunity comes along. If and when that day comes, it has the potential for becoming a "watershed moment" in your walk with Him, as you face the challenge of whether or not you're willing take a leap of faith *right into His arms!* It will also really help you "nail down" whom it is you're really working for. Remember this: it is much worse to stay too long once your work is finished, just going through the motions, waiting for another church to come along. Here, you run the risk of losing what has been gained in the years of ministry you've invested with these people, as they will soon see that your heart is no longer in your work with them. I have seen several other pastors, a couple of them dear friends of mine, who tried to "run out the clock," just marking time until something comfortable came along. These were pastorates that did not end well. If you truly love your people, you will want to be sure to leave on a positive note and not "ride the church down." We are examples to our flocks of what it is to live by faith. This is true of us, *coming and going*. It would be a wasteful tragedy for a pilot, instead of landing the plane at the end of the journey, to just circle the field until all the fuel is gone and then crash with all his passengers. One thing Jennifer and I have learned is this: The Lord will always provide, though His timing does not always coincide with ours. The times we've struggled between pastorates have in retrospect been some of the most productive times in our lives, with respect to the development of our faith. It really has been truly amazing how He has always taken care of us in every way.

Now we finally arrive at the question: How then can I know when it is time to conclude a pastorate? The first thing I would say, though it may sound trite, is that *only the Lord* can tell you when it is time. Again, we are brought face-to-face with the necessity of cultivating and protecting a close walk with Him. Whenever you must grapple with any kind of major life decision, there are usually many other voices in addition to His which are screaming and clamoring to get and hold your attention, each trying to get you to follow a different course of action. The devil usually "beats a drum and blows a horn" with everything he tries to do, while our Lord, who can certainly "answer by fire" when it suits His purpose, usually quietly goes about His plan. We need to be sure to listen for our Great Shepherd's voice and be sure we're following Him. Give yourself time for extended prayer about what He would have you to do if you're considering making some kind of ministry move. Often, the frustrations of one's present situation can lead to the assumption, "It must be time to move on," when perhaps your best work may still lie ahead. Your time with Him will help you sort through your combined feelings, anxieties, frustrations, and dreams. None of the pastorates with which I have been entrusted went exactly the way I thought they would when I started. The congregation that exploded with the most growth was also a church I was reluctant to become pastor of—until the Lord convinced me I should. One of the things to consider is whether or not you've realistically done all you can for this congregation. If you stay on, will you be able to lead them forward, or will you just be "marking time?" Do you believe you have fulfilled your stewardship here? Have you finished the job He sent you to do? Jesus set the bar quite high when in His prayer He told the Father, "I have finished the work which thou gavest me to do" (John 17:4). I must admit that many tasks in my life have been left undone, halfway done, or poorly done. However, it is important that we make a thorough and realistic assessment of our work before we "call it good" and move on. What will the condition of the flock be if you leave now? Will they be in a better situation than they were in when you came? Will you be leaving things "in a mess" for the next pastor to clean up?   Do you have ministry projects underway that will "die on the vine" if you abandon them now? Surely you will always see that there is more that needs to be done, but can you realistically expect that *you* will be able to get it accomplished? Are *you* still needed here? Do not forget that being called to shepherd a flock is a call to serve *them,* so if they still have needs that *you* are equipped to meet, that is an important clue. As we said in an earlier chapter, when the right church comes along, you will "just know." The same thing will be true when it is time to move on. Seek the Lord out and listen to Him. What is He calling you to do? He will not steer you wrong!

How to Conclude a Pastorate

During my years as a carpenter building houses with my father, there was a fine plumber named Alvin who many times would be installing such things as faucets and plumbing fixtures during the final days of construction as my father and I put the finishing touches on the nearly completed house. During the process each time, we would hear Alvin say at least once, "There's a lotta work in finishin' up a job!" He was right every time, for it seemed that when it would take about another week to finish, it would often take twice that long to get everything done, so the house would be as nearly perfect as we could make it for the new owner. The same thing applies in the ministry.

When the time arrives for you to finish, you owe it to the Lord, your people, and yourself to leave everything as completely finished as you possibly can. Of course, there will be ongoing things that come up during the course of congregational life. For example, I've conducted funerals and administered baptisms during the last few days of a pastorate. However, it is advisable to do your very best to see that the machinery is in place within the congregation to help them have a smooth transition into and hopefully through the interim period until the next pastor arrives. Different individual congregations and churches of different denominations often have different processes for this. Some churches in their by-laws specify, for example, that perhaps the deacons will have charge of securing pulpit supply and perhaps selecting the members of the "Interim Pastor Committee" and perhaps also the "Pastor Search Committee." In a church such as this, where the process is fairly well defined, you may not need to do much, other than be available as a resource person, should they seek your advice with regard to suggesting some qualified personnel who might be able to provide temporary ministry assistance after you're gone. Be careful though, for the moment you turn in your resignation the dynamics will change—you will be "a lame duck" from that moment on. From the time you resign, it's as though your leadership has shifted from "high gear" into "neutral" as you hopefully "glide" in together for a landing. Again, this is one facet of the pastorate where you indeed must "fly by the seat of your pants!" Every congregational situation is different, and you must be careful to try to "keep the wings level" as you descend—you must walk a fine line between staying in tune with what is needed from you and also allowing things to come to a natural and smooth completion of your journey together.

Be aware that the Adversary will also be at work, especially during this time, trying to "grab the controls and crash the plane," and he always has a few people who will want to rise up and "seize power" as you try to finish up your work. Do not allow yourself to be lured into some controversy or power struggle that will divert your attention from your present God-called role of "landing the plane!" More than once there have been would-be "power players" in churches I served who were just waiting to "grab the wheel" once I had announced my resignation. No doubt you will already know beforehand who those people are likely to be, for they are probably the same "Korahs, Dathans, and Abirams" with whom you've had dealings in the past. Remember, Moses allowed the Lord to deal with them in his day (Numbers 16), and hopefully you've been doing the same thing during your tenure. Don't let yourself be pulled into a controversy now as you finish--This could turn what should be a celebration into a tragedy. The Lord can handle this— *so let Him!*

Do not forget that when you leave *the congregation* will have to make their own choice as to what their direction will be in the future. What they do once "the plane is on the ground" is not your call. As you depart like Moses going up Nebo to meet whatever He has next for you, they must be fully entrusted to the capable hands of the Great Shepherd, who will also continue to work His plan for them. Try your best to "tie up all the loose ends" insofar as you can, and when you leave, *leave!* Make a clean break with them as you move on, so they (and you) can go through a healthy period of grief that will solidify for everyone the value of your time together. As with fresh milk, give it time to settle, and "the cream will rise to the top!" In the years to come, even some of the people who were "burrs under your saddle" are likely to recognize much of the good that came to them through your time together. If you can finish in a positive manner, the "taste" of you that lingers in the congregation will be both sweet and wholesome, and you will have become a strong link in their chain of leadership onto which the next pastor can connect and hopefully build upon what God has done through you.

www.ingramcontent.com/pod-product-compliance
Lightning Source LLC
Chambersburg PA
CBHW031259060726
47590CB00003B/979